FAST & NATURAL CUISINE

A COMPLETE GUIDE TO EASY VEGETARIAN AND SEAFOOD COOKING

FAST & NATURAL CUISINE

A COMPLETE GUIDE TO EASY VEGETARIAN AND SEAFOOD COOKING

by Susann Geiskopf and Mindy Toomay

Illustrated by Chris Rose-Merkle

Library of Congress Cataloging in Publication Data

Geiskopf, Susann and Toomay, Melinda
    Fast & Natural Cuisine: A complete Guide to Easy Vegetarian and Seafood Cooking

    Bibliography: p.
    Includes index.
    1. Vegetarian cookery.   2. Cookery (Seafood)   3. Cookery (Natural foods)
    I. Toomay, Mindy, 1951-   II. Title.   III. Title; Fast and natural cuisine.
TX 837.G38   1983   641.5'636   83-61867
ISBN 0-930356-38-1 (pbk.)

Copyright © Susann Geiskopf and Melinda Toomay 1983

Illustrated by Chris Rose-Merkle
Illustrations © Quicksilver Productions 1983

2   3   4   5   6   7   8   9   95   94   93   92   91   90   89   88   87

INTERNATIONAL STANDARD BOOK NUMBER: 0-930356-38-1

LIBRARY OF CONGRESS CATALOG CARD NUMBER: 83-061867

Published by Quicksilver Productions, P.O. Box 340, Ashland, Oregon 97520

TABLE OF CONTENTS

Foreword 9

Chapter 1. Mindful Eating 11

    A Choice in the Matter 12
    Food as Fuel 12
    Crash Course in Mindful Eating 14
    Convenience Cooking 15

Chapter 2. Getting Started 19

    The Right Kitchen Tools 20

    Absolute Essentials 20
    Almost Essentials 21
    Elite Essentials 22
    Extravagant Unessentials 22

    Foods to Keep on Hand 23

    General Shopping Hints 23
    "Foods to Keep on Hand" list 24
    Stocking Up Naturally 25

Chapter 3. Appetizers 37

Chapter 4. Salads and Dressings 53

Chapter 5. Soups 71

Chapter 6. Sauces 85

TABLE OF CONTENTS

Chapter 7. Vegetable Accompaniments 97

Chapter 8. Grain and Pasta Accompaniments 111

Chapter 9. Main Courses 119
    Vegetables Main Courses 120
    Pasta Main Courses 134
    Tofu Main Courses 142
    Fish and Seafood Main Courses 150

Chapter 10. Baked Goods and Sweets 163

Chapter 11. Morning Meals 187

Chapter 12. Holiday Delights 203

Chapter 13. Beverages 213

Chapter 14. Menu Planning 221

Appendices: Charts and Lists 229
    Weights and measures 229
    Abbreviations used 230
    Equivalents 230
    Metric conversion table 231
    Oven temperatures 231
    Storage temperatures 231
    Tricks of the Trade 232
    Recommended reading 234
    Glossary of terms 235

Index 239

Authors 255

FOREWORD

It's spring, and we've escaped to a country inn in the hills of California's wine-growing region. Against a backdrop of oaks, madrones, and digger pines, daffodils and irises glow in the light of the setting sun. With the croaking of frogs as background music, we discuss the purpose of our book.

For both of us, the last few years have seen a shift in emphasis and direction. We once had the time for a thorough investigation into personal nutrition. Now our lives are jam-packed with careers, relationships, and special projects—all the activities that fill the hours of a day. We discovered that in our separate kitchens we were co-evolving to adapt to the quicker pace—developing new food combinations and recipes that maintain our standards of good nutrition, yet fit into busy lives. We decided to share our recent discoveries with friends.

We hope we can help you discover that the creation of healthful and appetizing meals is not mystical or complicated, nor does it require a major time commitment. You needn't ever grind wheat into flour, or make your own yogurt, or soak soybeans for hours (although you may someday choose to do so). All our simple style of cooking requires is some information, some practice, and a willingness to experience something new.

We present, then, a cookbook for people like us, whose lives demand a vitality that only sound nutrition can provide but who don't want to sacrifice leisurely sunsets.

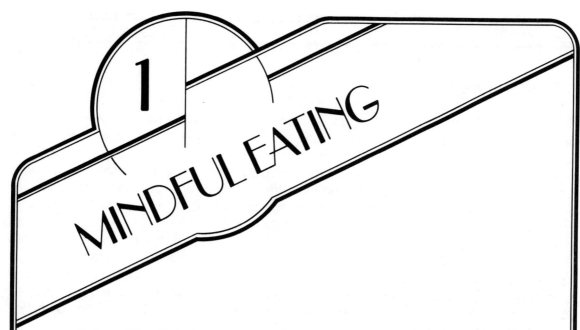

1

MINDFUL EATING

Eating. We all do it, most of us three times a day. We all budget a good portion of our time and money for it. We eat because we're truly hungry, or for sensual gratification, or to fill uncharted time, or just to be social. A lot of us enjoy it, but we seldom think much about it. Important as eating is in our lives, for many it is a totally mindless activity.

Growing numbers of us, however, are choosing to take a more mindful approach to diet. Perhaps the change is triggered by an expanding waistline, or a bout of ill health or sluggishness, or an article in a magazine, or dining with new friends and learning that they're vegetarians. For whatever reasons, we are deciding to pay more attention to what and how we eat.

A Choice in the Matter

Our eating habits are influenced by countless factors, such as media advertising, clever packaging, and the way our mothers used to cook. Because much of this influence is subliminal, our personal eating styles are often developed unconsciously. The greatest degree of choice many of us exercise about the food we eat is selecting something from a restaurant menu. Once considered, however, the options are seen to be as various as wildflowers in a meadow. We don't have to pigeonhole ourselves (as carnivores or vegetarians, for instance) and live with the limitations those labels imply. Adherence to an inflexible diet concept isn't necessary. By simply beginning to accept responsibility for our choices and tuning into our bodies' signals, we can develop a personal eating style which need not be exactly like anyone else's. And even when we become committed to a new food philosophy there can always be room for an occasional spontaneous indulgence. If you have the urge to eat a hot fudge sundae whenever the moon is full, you should enjoy it without even a twinge of guilt.

Food as Fuel

Nutritional research has taught us that the quality of our lives can be enhanced by simple changes in diet. Many psychological and physiological diseases have been linked to a deficiency (or, in rare cases, over abundance) of some particular nutrient. But don't feel compelled to scour the medical journals or to embark on a lifelong study of human metabolism, although such undertakings can be enlightening. Your new philosophy about diet and health can be based on the simple realization that what you eat makes a difference.

Food is the body's fuel, and some foods are better fuels than others. The foods we eat determine energy production, so if your goal is to maintain a positive attitude and productive lifestyle, it is worthwhile to pay attention to how you nourish yourself. A well-rounded diet is essential. All the nutrients we consume work as a team to produce good health. It makes sense to familiarize ourselves with the roles of various nutritional elements so we can make informed choices about what we eat. We offer here some basic facts about foods and their functions.

Sugars enter the bloodstream quickly—different sugars at different rates. When thinking of sugars, remember that we get the most usable sugars from natural sources such as fruits and raw dairy products, not from sweeteners. Plain white table sugar, for instance, is a highly refined substance with no value as a food. It is solid sucrose and enters the blood too quickly, creating a "sugar rush" that overworks our metabolic processes. (When fully digested, everything we eat becomes a form of sugar called glucose, which is the "energy producer" carried in the bloodstream.)

Proteins and complex carbohydrates—grains, for example—are metabolized more slowly than sugars, so they help to sustain a high energy level between meals. Most Americans think of meat as the only source of complete protein (thanks, in part, to the Five Food Groups). But grains, eggs, dairy products, fish, and soy products such as tofu and miso all provide amino acids, which are the building blocks of proteins. When a variety of these foods is eaten daily, the amino acids can combine to form complete proteins. There is a great deal of talk these days about the real role of proteins in health maintenance, and many experts suggest that adults in America—meat-eaters in particular—eat **too much** protein. So the vegetarian who eats a well-balanced diet need not worry about getting insufficient protein.

Vegetables, too, provide small amounts of some amino acids, plus the vitamins and minerals our bodies utilize in innumerable ways. Many raw vegetables provide bulk and roughage, which help to keep the stomach and intestines functioning properly. This is why salads should play an important role in your daily diet.

The fats provided by such foods as unrefined, raw vegetable oils, dairy products, and seeds and nuts perform the essential function of bonding nutrients together so that they can travel through the bloodstream. They also help lubricate the digestive and eliminative systems and provide us with essential vitamins.

A meal consisting of all these elements will begin to break down and enter the bloodstream almost immediately and will continue to supply us with blood sugar (energy) for about four hours. Give your body enough time to assimilate a meal fully before you eat again. The result will be a dependable reserve of energy and a feeling of lightness and vitality.

Crash Course in Mindful Eating

The mindful approach to diet involves not only a shift for many of us to different foods, but also a new attentiveness to how we actually consume them. Fad foods and crash diets are usually ineffective in our attempts to achieve a dependable energy supply and ideal weight. You're likely to go farther toward these goals by selecting healthful foods and making a few simple adjustments to your eating habits.

▶ Eat your protein course first, when the stomach is empty. Hydrochloric acid is necessary for digesting protein and is diluted when vegetables are eaten first. Many stomach and colon problems could be averted by making this simple adjustment. Eat a salad—it's important—but eat it as the last course.

▶ Eat slowly. Place only a small amount of food on your plate and on your fork, and put your fork down between bites so that you don't slip into the "shoveling" syndrome.

▶ Eat only when you're really hungry, but don't wait to eat until you're famished—then you're more likely to wolf down the meal.

▶ Chew well. Digestion actually begins in your mouth while you're chewing. Many digestive disturbances happen because all the work is left to the stomach.

▶ Don't keep eating until you're absolutely stuffed at each meal. Since it takes a while for your fullness to be felt, try to wait about twenty minutes before you have a second helping, to see whether you're really still hungry.

▶ Avoid drinking beverages during meals: liquids dilute the enzyme-rich juices that digest food. A light beverage at least half an hour before meals, however, will quench your thirst and may help to prevent overeating.

▶ A meal that is fully enjoyable looks, smells, and tastes good. Breathe deeply during your meal to get the greatest possible satisfaction from every bite you take. Eating should be a special event—set a nice table in a favorite spot. Make mealtime a time to relax and enjoy.

▶ Don't eat on your feet, or idly in front of the television, or while reading. You are less aware at these times of just how much food you are consuming.

▶ Don't eat (or keep yourself from eating) to reward or punish yourself (or anyone else). Your weight and your eating habits, and the power to change them, are yours.

▶ Yes, exercise is vital. Energy-in must be balanced by energy-out or we'll get fat and sluggish. If motivation is a problem for you, try exercising with a dependable friend, or make new friends by joining an exercise class or health club.

Mindful eating is a continuing process, because our diets must adapt to changes in activity level, climate, and season, and to metabolic changes as we age. So keep paying attention.

Lest we sound like dull and inflexible headmistresses, we admit that a bottle of wine is never unwelcome at our dinner tables!

Convenience Cooking

When time for food is limited, convenience becomes an important consideration. But **convenience** is often a misapplied word. Did you know, for instance, that steaming fresh vegetables takes no more time than cooking frozen ones?

Once you make the move toward more fresh foods in the diet, a little experimentation will convince you that they're as simple to prepare as foods from cans and boxes. You may have to accustom yourself to using different cooking techniques and ingredients, and you may eventually decide to look for a grocery where the foods are always fresh. But once the changes are made, new routines will evolve that are as convenient and comfortable as your old ones.

In your fresh approach to cooking, allow just a little time for planning a meal. A few moments spent reading through a recipe and mentally organizing procedures will save you from frustrated feelings and scorched pans. It's worth the minute it takes to gather all your ingredients together so that everything's at your fingertips. With quick-preparation dishes like those in this book, the time you spend rummaging in your spice cupboard can take you away from the stove at a critical moment, sometimes with sad results. There is great pleasure in literally surrounding yourself with seemingly unrelated ingredients, then combining them into a nourishing gastronomical delight. It can help you experience cooking as the creative adventure people say it is. Perhaps the Mad Chemist in you will be inspired to concoct sensational recipes all your own.

Along with pre-preparation time-savers, there are some post-preparation devices to enhance the kitchen experience. Few people enjoy cleaning the kitchen, so make it easier on yourself or your helpers by "thinking neat." Keep a sponge handy to immediately wipe up spills; rinse or soak dishes and utensils immediately after using them; and try to take just a moment to put all ingredients—spices, cooking oil, and so on—away before sitting down to eat. Simply adjust your attitude and replace any sloppy habits with neater ones, then relax and enjoy the time you spend in the kitchen.

With an interest in good nutrition, the right tools, and a pantry well-stocked with natural instead of processed foods, you can put together wonderful meals in a flash. The next chapter will provide the details to get you started on your new "convenience" kitchen.

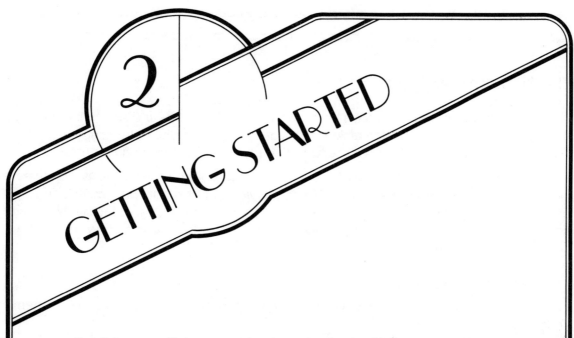

2 GETTING STARTED

Confidence, efficiency, and enjoyment in the kitchen are within every-one's grasp. If you are already a good creative cook, this chapter may not teach you anything new, but it could become your favorite information bank. We've brought together in one place the most useful facts gleaned over the years from our own experiences as cooks.

If the craft of cooking is new to you, then your education begins here. We don't expect you to follow our instructions blindly; we give you the hows and whys to make your lessons easy and enjoyable. Even the finest cooks are always learning, from their successes and their failures. It's all part of the process.

The Right Kitchen Tools

Wooden spoons beckon from a tin on the stove; jars of herbs and spices line one wall; sharp knives glisten in a wooden rack; patchwork potholders decorate a cupboard door. Tools can be great time savers if we keep them ready to use and at our fingertips.

The cooking experience is more fun in warm and colorful surroundings, so create a kitchen you'll enjoy spending time in and furnish it with tools that suit your interests and level of skill. Reflecting on how our kitchens are evolving, we've developed a graduated guide to help with the task of choosing appropriate tools. After all, if a trowel works best for planting bulbs, why use a teaspoon?

Absolute Essentials

If you're equipping your kitchen from scratch, get these things first—you'll need them if you're going to cook anything.

Good pans are essential. We most frequently use 8-inch and 12-inch cast-iron skillets (with lids), and we prefer stainless steel or enameled cast iron for saucepans. One-, two-, and three-quart saucepans are the handiest sizes. Mixing bowls may double as serving bowls—glass, ceramic, and stainless steel are all good; 1-quart and 2½-quart sizes will serve most purposes.

Cast-iron skillet
Saucepans, including a double boiler
Mixing bowls
Wooden spoons
Measuring cups and spoons
Cutting board
Corkscrew
Can opener
Large vegetable knife or cleaver

Paring knife
Stainless steel spatula
Colander
Eggbeater

Airtight containers and labels
    for herbs and spices
Potholders
Grater

Almost Essentials

When you're ready to expand your repertoire of cooking skills and recipes, you'll want to acquire more varied and specialized tools.

Look for glass or cast-iron baking pans and dishes, because they distribute heat most evenly. You'll find 1½-, 2-, and 3-quart casserole dishes most useful.

Casserole dishes with lids
Pie plate
Cookie sheet
Muffin tin
Bread pan (loaf pan)
Rolling pin
Mouli™ Julienne*
Blender
Stainless steel slotted spoon
Electric mixer

Stainless steel wire whisk
Rubber spatula
Flour sifter
Garlic press
Kitchen timer

* For those otherwise time-consuming tasks such as shredding cabbage and grating hard cheeses, the Mouli™ is a wonder. This is a French hand-crank grater that comes with several different-sized grating discs. An inexpensive and amazingly efficient tool!

Elite Essentials

These are almost extras, but for versatility and ease of preparation you'll want these kitchen frills.

Pressure cooker
Omelette and/or crêpe pan
Wok
Bundt pan
Springform pan
Nutcracker
Mortar and pestle
Pepper grinder
Waffle iron
Toaster or toaster oven
Juicing dish
Small strainer with a handle
Salad spinner
Funnel
Sharpening stone
Cutlery

Egg timer
Baskets, jars, and other storage containers
Spoon jar
Cotton or linen towels
Pastry cutter

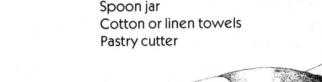

Extravagant Unessentials

Just a word about the fanciest of all kitchen tools. Food processors, pasta machines, and the like are for the experienced cook who wants to play with these newfangled kitchen gadgets. They're fun and may save time, but they're not for everyone.

None of the quick and simple recipes in this book requires the use of complex appliances—you'll find you can be a good, efficient cook without relying on them. Hands-on experience and enthusiasm for the simple tasks will help you develop a working knowledge of ingredients and procedures. As you develop favorite culinary pursuits, you may want to acquire more specialized tools.

Foods to Keep on Hand

It is stimulating and rewarding to become familiar with foods you haven't used before—it's like making new friends. In the beginning, shopping will take more thought and perhaps a little more time. Once you've adapted to your modified shopping list, however, your trips to the market will take no longer than they used to. Your reward will be more nutritious, quicker meals.

General Shopping Hints

Shop at a market that you feel is conscientious in its buying practices. Whenever possible, shop at local produce markets and stands for the freshest produce and eggs, and talk to the growers themselves about their farming practices. Residues of chemical fertilizers and pesticides remain in produce and may contribute to health problems. Choose organically grown foods whenever possible.

If you buy canned or packaged foods, read the labels. The presence of synthetic ingredients such as artificial colors and flavors tells you that the manufacturer is trying to make something that you **wouldn't** want to eat, look and taste like something you **would.** Preservatives are added to foods to prolong shelf life, primarily for the convenience of the manufacturer and the grocer. Shop a little more frequently, buying fresh and unadulterated foods—it's worth the time.

Some foods that are particularly perishable, notably dairy products, are stamped with a date after which their freshness is not guaranteed. This date will let you know which carton of milk on the shelf is freshest.

Pretty packaging is often a gimmick used to entice you to spend your money on empty calories. Fresh foods will always be your best buy. If your shopping basket is usually full of boxes, canned goods, and frozen foods, begin to think about alternatives.

"Foods to Keep on Hand"

Grains:

Bulghur (cracked wheat)
Bran
Brown rice
Cornmeal
Millet
Popcorn
Whole wheat pastry flour

Seeds:

Sesame seeds
Sunflower seeds

Nuts and Butters:

Peanut butter
Tahini (sesame butter)
Fresh nuts in shells

Bread and pasta products:

Assorted crackers
Egg noodles
English muffins
Whole-grain bread
Whole-grain pastas

Dairy products:

Assorted cheeses
Butter
Buttermilk
Half-and-half
Milk
Parmesan cheese
Sour cream
Yogurt

Soy products:

Miso
Tamari soy sauce
Tofu

Basic produce:

Carrots
Celery
Garlic
Lemons
Lettuce
Parsley
Potatoes
Onions (bulb and green)

Basic herbs and spices:

Basil
Bay leaves
Black pepper
Caraway seeds
Cayenne pepper
Celery seeds
Chili powder
Cinnamon
Cloves
Cumin
Curry powder
Dill weed
Ginger
Mustard, ground
Nutmeg
Oregano
Poppy seeds
Sea salt
Tarragon
Thyme

Other basics:

Eggs
Olive oil
Sesame oil
Apple cider vinegar
Wine vinegars
Honey
Maple syrup
Dijon mustard
Catsup
Baking powder
Baking soda

Arrowroot powder
Bakon yeast
Brewer's yeast
Pure vanilla extract
Carob powder
Marmite™
Vegetable broth powder
Fruit juices
Dried fruits

Canned and bottled products:

Black olives (whole)
Capers
Green chiles (whole)
Tomato paste
Tomato purée
Whole tomatoes

Stocking up Naturally

Grains are the seeds of certain plants wrapped in a protective shell with all the nutrients required to start the seeds growing if they get planted. They are inexpensive sources of important vitamins, minerals, and proteins. They also provide an important cleansing function in the digestive and eliminative systems.

Grains must be chewed thoroughly if they are to be digested properly, so most are cooked or soaked to facilitate chewing. Many are quick-cooking. Whole grains are most nutritious and can be enjoyed daily. Store them in a dry, cool, dark place in tightly closed containers. Most whole-grains will keep indefinitely; every once in a while check them for pests; if you find any, discard the grains. Whole-grain bread, crackers, and pasta are good on occasion for variety. Unless prepared at home, these processed foods are at least somewhat devitalized, so use them infrequently.

25

Breads

When you do use breads, choose whole-grain varieties without preservatives or additives—the label shouldn't list ingredients you wouldn't have at home. Sprouted grains are wonderfully sweet and wholesome tasting, and the breads made from them are delicious. Store bread in an airtight bag in a dry, dark, cool place (like a breadbox), or in the refrigerator. If tightly wrapped and sealed, breads can be stored in the freezer for up to three months with no loss in flavor or nutritional value.

Flours

Whole wheat flour is finely milled whole wheat kernels ("whole" means including the wheat germ and the bran). Whole wheat pastry flour is generally milled from a soft variety of wheat and is preferable where a fine texture is desired, as in pastry, and as a thickening agent in sauces. Flours made from other grains or legumes (such as rice, rye, or soybeans) are great for variety or if you are allergic to wheat. Combine different flours in a recipe when possible, because the different amino acids may combine to form complete proteins.

Look for "stone-ground" on the label. It means the flour was ground using old-fashioned millstones with grooves that allow air to circulate to keep the grain cool, which prevents rancidity and the attendant loss of nutrients. The more modern processing method uses giant rollers that speed over the grain, creating excessive heat, and this destroys much of its food value.

Pasta

Many varieties of whole-grain pasta are available—wheat, corn, rice, buckwheat, etc. Some include powdered sesame seed, spinach, or artichoke. Check the label for undesirable additives and preservatives. For a special nourishing treat, invite a few friends over for a simple feast, and spend an hour one morning making your own noodles. The noodles will be dry and ready to use by evening, and your friends will feel pampered.

Dairy Products

Lots of us are hooked on dairy products. They add richness and variety to our diets and supply a complete protein. Be aware of the disadvantages of pasteurized milk products, however. Modern processing and pasteurization of milk removes valuable nutrients and adds chemicals (sometimes even recognized carcinogens) in order to prolong shelf life. Investigate certified raw milk producers in your area. Most health-food stores offer certified raw products.

Cultured milk products can be invaluable to good digestion, because they contain friendly bacteria that work in the stomach and intestines. The culturing process changes lactose (milk sugar) to a more easily assimilated substance, lactic acid. Since many of America's major health hazards are related to unhealthy digestion, it pays to acquire a taste for plain yogurt (add your own fruit, if you like), raw buttermilk, ricotta, and low-fat cottage cheeses. Eat them regularly.

If you are allergic to cow's milk or can't digest it easily, you can usually substitute soy milk, or even water, successfully when a recipe calls for milk. Goat's milk, which is alkaline and easily digestible, is preferable to cow's milk, especially if you have digestion problems or are prone to allergies. Again, look for raw goat's milk products. Most people have to develop a taste for it ("it tastes so goaty!"). Cheese and yogurt made from goat's milk are generally mild in flavor.

Cheese is usually 20—25 percent milk protein by bulk, and is high in calcium, phosphorus, and vitamins A and B. Many cheeses are high in fat, though, so it's a good idea to limit your intake. Pasteurized processed cheeses (sometimes called "cheese food") are nutritionally worthless and have no place in a high-energy diet. Best are raw milk cheeses, preferably made without rennet (an enzyme found in the stomachs of cows, used in cheese-making as an unnecessary coagulant). Always check the label to make sure the cheese doesn't contain chemical additives or preservatives. A small quantity of cheese can be stored for a long period in the refrigerator if it's tightly wrapped to avoid dryness and hardening. A cheese will age (or ripen) if stored in a cool, dry place. Any mold that forms may be cut away—in most cases it will not have affected the goodness of the cheese (in fact, sometimes it adds to the flavor!). Most cheeses taste best at room temperature.

Eggs

Eggs have received bad press in recent years because of the cholesterol scare. Although eggs are high in cholesterol, they are also high in lecithin, a substance that appears to act as a homogenizing agent in the blood, breaking down fats and aiding in their assimilation, so eggs are very well balanced nutritionally.

Regular supermarket-variety eggs are often heavily contaminated with estrogen, antibiotics, and even some suspected carcinogens. Fertile eggs (those that a rooster helped to make), from hens that have been organically fed and allowed to run free and scratch, taste better and are nutritionally superior. These high-quality eggs are considered by many nutritionists to supply the most perfect package of nutrients for human health. Because they are a rich food, eat eggs in moderation—two per day is probably overdoing it. Remember that many baked goods, casseroles, and sauces add "hidden" eggs to our diets.

Freshness is crucial. Buy eggs you know are fresh and store them in the refrigerator no longer than a week. Because eggshells are porous, it's a good idea to store them in a container (their original carton will do).

Nuts and Seeds

Nuts are excellent sources of protein, B vitamins, phosphorus, iron, and calcium. Because of the high oil content of most kinds of nuts, it is best to use them rather sparingly as crunchy and flavorful additions to other foods, or a few at a time as a snack.

Nuts should be purchased still tightly sealed in their shells, as rancidity occurs quickly when their oils are exposed to air. Nuts in their shells will last for months when stored in a cool, dry place in a ventilated container. Occasionally spend half an hour shelling your favorite nuts so that they will be at your fingertips when you want them. Small quantities of shelled nuts can be stored in airtight containers in the refrigerator for day-to-day use, or they can be frozen for longer periods.

Most nuts can be enjoyed either raw or cooked. Peanuts are easier to digest when lightly roasted. To roast nuts, spread them over the bottom of a cast-iron skillet over high heat and shake frequently until a wonderful nutty aroma lets you know they are done (about 10 minutes).

The freshest and tastiest nuts are those you gather yourself very soon after they've dropped from the tree. Remove their hulls if they are still attached, and leave the nuts spread out on a dry clean surface for a few weeks to dry. Store them as described above.

Many seeds are full of flavor, nutrients, and oils. Select seeds carefully; rancidity is not uncommon. If you can find a bulk supplier, you can smell and taste before you buy. A fishy smell or bitter taste indicates rancidity. If you must buy seeds prepackaged, look for ones that are raw, unsalted, and still have their shells.

When buying nut and seed butters, read and compare labels. The best butters contain nothing but the nut or seed itself. Oil separation is a natural occurrence—when you're ready to use the butter, just stir the contents of the jar to blend it again. The best peanut butter is the kind you grind yourself, so look for a natural-food store or supermarket that keeps a grinder and fresh nuts on hand—remember to check the nuts for rancidity before you grind them. Sesame seed butter, often sold as **tahini,** is a delicious alternative to nut butters. Nut and seed butters keep well when stored in airtight containers in the refrigerator; they spoil quickly when exposed to light, warmth, and air.

Oils

Fats are essential to good nutrition and the production of energy. Not all kinds of fat are equally valuable, however. Seed and vegetable oils, in moderation, can be a wonderful addition to your diet. Lard, shortening, and hydrogenated margarines, on the other hand, may adversely affect health. **Hydrogenation,** the process by which liquid oils are rendered solid, subjects oils to high heat, intense pressure, and chemical adulteration. Since heat and air are major causes of rancidity, hydrogenation creates a product which bears little resemblance, in nutritional value or taste, to the fresh oil from which it was made. The new product is just conveniently fluffy or hard. Notably, lecithin, a vital participant in fat metabolism, is destroyed in the hydrogenation process. Vitamins A, B, E, and K are also lost when oils are refined or hydrogenated. Studies have shown that consumption of rancid oils can destroy the body's existing supplies of these vital nutrients.

We recommend raw, cold-pressed olive and sesame seed oils. Buy them in small quantities (perhaps pints) and store in dark, tightly sealed bottles in the refrigerator. If you can find a bulk supplier, all the better, since you can smell and taste the oil before you buy. Good oils smell like the food from which they're pressed. Rancid oils smell fishy and taste bitter or flat.

Herbs and Spices

Herbs and spices add variety and complex flavor to foods. Also, many herbs are reputed to stimulate the flow of digestive enzymes.

Herbs and spices may be used either fresh or dried. In general, dried herbs impart a stronger flavor than their fresh counterparts; when substituting one for the other in a recipe, adjust the amount accordingly. Fresh herbs can be picked right off the plant and tossed into the cooking pot. Often the leaves are stripped from the stems and the woody stems are discarded. Fresh herbs will keep for a few days in the refrigerator if they are stored in an airtight container. Freshly picked parsley stays fresh for a few days when placed, like a bouquet of flowers, in a glass of water on the kitchen counter, out of direct sunlight.

Of the dried herbs and spices, powders are more perishable than the crumbled variety. Store all dried seasonings in tightly closed opaque containers (or in the dark). When adding a dried herb to a dish, crush quickly between your palms first to release the aroma and flavor.

Culinary Herb Blends

You can purchase commercial herb blends at any supermarket, but for the freshest and most potent flavors look for a bulk herb supplier in your area and try mixing your own. Mixing your own has the advantage of helping you to learn about and develop your personal tastes (you may want to put the emphasis of your Italian mix on oregano rather than basil, for instance). It's satisfying to learn what each herb looks and smells like; even a little familiarity with some basic seasonings can increase your repertoire of special dishes a hundredfold. Whether you choose the ready-made variety or blend your own concoctions, do explore the endless possibilities herbs provide for quickly creating a variety of flavors.

Here are some of our favorite herb and spice combinations and some suggestions about the kinds of dishes they enhance.

Italian seasoning:

3 tsp basil
2 tsp oregano
2 tsp dried parsley
1 tsp rosemary

Use for:

Tomato sauce
Dressings for green salad
Marinades

Curry concoction:

3 tsp ground ginger
2 tsp crushed mustard seeds
3 tsp crushed coriander
3 tsp ground turmeric
1 tsp ground cloves
2 tsp ground cumin
1 tsp cayenne
1½ tsp ground cinnamon

Use for:

Vegetable stir-fries, soups and stews, rice, dressings for green salads, cream sauces

Chinese 5-spice:

Equal parts, ground:

Anise
Fennel
Licorice root
Ginger
Cinnamon
Cloves

Use for:

Vegetable stir-fries
Cakes, cookies, quick breads
Dressings for fruit salads

Gomasio:

Grind together:

1 part sea salt
5 parts sesame seeds

Use for:

Fresh steamed vegetables
Tofu dishes
Salads
Soups

Pumpkin pie blend:

1 tsp ground ginger
4 tsp ground cinnamon
1 tsp ground nutmeg
½ tsp ground cloves

Use for:

Cakes, cookies, quick breads
Yams, sweet potatoes, winter squashes
Even pumpkin pie!

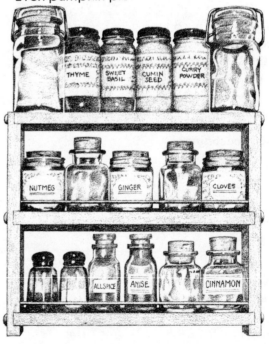

Soy Products

Tofu is a cultured soybean product; it is often called **bean curd**. A wonderful source of low-calorie protein, its bland flavor places it among the most versatile of foods. Simply dice or crumble it, then add to soups, salads, stir-fries, casseroles, or desserts. Any sauce, sweet or spicy, will enhance its flavor. Tofu can be purchased in water-filled containers at many supermarkets. If the water is changed daily, it will keep in the refrigerator for several days. If your grocer doesn't carry tofu, ask him to order it, or buy it at an Asian specialty-food or health-food store.

Miso, also called **soybean paste**, is a fermented seasoning made from soybeans, a grain (usually rice), water, and salt. A staple in Chinese and Japanese cooking for centuries, it is finally taking its place in the kitchens of Western cooks. Miso is high in protein and in salt. Mixed with a little water to create a smooth paste, it can be added to your favorite soup for a richer-tasting broth. It is also a delicious addition to salad dressings, sauces, and sandwich spreads. Look for miso in plastic tubs at a natural-foods supermarket or an Asian specialty-food store. It will keep indefinitely in a cool, dry place.

Soy sauce is made from soybeans, water, salt, and often with wheat. It is naturally fermented and aged for a rich and savory flavor. Soy sauce can be used as a nutritionally superior salt substitute in many foods where a savory flavor is desired. Use it in soups, sauces, sautés, and casseroles, and don't neglect it as a salad seasoning—it can become the secret ingredient that makes your salads especially tasty.

Most supermarket soy sauce is a poor substitute for the real thing. It is often not fermented or aged, and it usually contains additives. It will be worth the effort to seek out a good soy sauce in an Asian specialty-food store or in a natural-foods store, where you may find **tamari**, the best soy sauce available. Soy sauce keeps indefinitely at room temperature.

Notes about Special Seasonings

We've singled out a few items that deserve special attention. They're no more nor less valuable than lots of other seasonings, but they are often overlooked or underappreciated.

Garlic is the undisputed king of culinary seasonings. Used with a gentle hand, it enhances other flavors and helps create full-bodied dishes. If you've never enjoyed garlic, you've probably been fed by an over-zealous garlic lover (and there are lots of us out there). Quite pungent when raw (as in salad dressings and marinades), it mellows considerably as it cooks. Garlic is sold in heads or bulbs; separate the individual cloves as you need them. Peeled garlic may be put through a garlic press (a great time-saving tool), or be chopped or minced.

Ginger root, a standard in Oriental cuisine, translates well to American cooking. It imparts a not-very-subtle flavor, so use it sparingly except where a distinct spiciness is desired. Pieces of the fresh root can be found in the produce section of most super-markets. Chop a piece off the root, and peel, then grate or mince it, before adding to soups, stews, stir-fries, or sauces.

Lemon is generally used where a refreshing zest is desired. Lemon juice by itself is the simplest seasoning for raw or cooked vegetables. The peel is a tangy addition to many dishes, and its bright yellow makes a cheerful garnish. Lemon can be used as the dominant flavoring in cakes, pies, cookies, and sauces. Its uses are almost limitless; some people even enjoy eating it raw, or dipped in honey!

Salt is essential in the diet, but you can eat too much of it and you can rely on it too heavily as a seasoning. Many foods naturally contain ample salt and are best seasoned more creatively or enjoyed as they are. When some sort of salty seasoning seems appropriate, we use unprocessed sea salt or tamari soy sauce instead of regular iodized table salt. For variety, particularly for table use, try sesame salt (sometimes called gomasio — see page 32) or an herb salt. All of these alternatives provide flavor and some nutritional value. If you're a heavy salt user, you would do well to cut down. As your palate becomes more sensitive you'll probably discover an abundance of new flavors that were previously masked by salt.

Pepper, an old standby, deserves a place in the spice cabinet; however, its indiscriminate use as a table seasoning is unfortunate. Too much pepper can numb your palate to the subtler flavors of fresh foods and herbs. Black pepper has been accused of irritating the stomach lining, whereas red pepper (cayenne) is reputed to aid digestion and purify the blood. Begin to substitute small quantities of cayenne for black pepper when you think pepper is indispensable.

Parsley is wonderful when fresh! A little chopped parsley is a great addition to vegetable and egg dishes, salads, and soups. Add it to a dish at the last moment so that its freshness is not ruined by overcooking. Don't miss its refreshing flavor because you leave it on the side of your plate as a garnish; next time, eat that sprig of parsley when you've finished your meal. It will sweeten the palate and stimulate the flow of digestive enzymes.

Green onions impart a more delicate flavor than bulb onions. The white end is very different in flavor and texture from the green shoots. You will find uses for both. When used raw, the crunchiness of green onions enlivens the texture of other foods, and their bright color makes a great garnish. Try them sliced over soups, salads, cooked vegetables, or eggs. They are also tasty when cooked along with rice and in vegetable stir-fries.

For a list of herb companions for vegetables see Chapter 7 (page 100).

3
APPETIZERS

Whenever people gather for casual fun, finger foods are likely to be part of the scene. They are a simple way to please our friends, whether they're served as the introduction that whets the appetite for a gastronomical feast or as a mini-feast all by themselves. People love to nibble, and it's a pleasure to provide something besides the standard chips and supermarket dip for their enjoyment.

Since appetizers often are especially quick to fix, you'll have more time to play with their presentation. Here's your opportunity to employ the little plates and bowls and baskets you seldom get to use. Colorful napkins and original garnishes help you express your delight in your friends' company.

Simplest Spreads

Blend small amounts of your favorite herb or spice (try curry powder, marjoram, caraway seed, or dill weed) with softened cream cheese. Transfer to a serving plate or bowl, and sprinkle with chili powder, paprika, or cayenne pepper for a colorful accent. These spreads will keep—and may improve—in the refrigerator for a few days, but serve at room temperature. For a crunchy variation, add chopped nuts or sunflower seeds.

Simplest Dips

Blend small amounts of minced onion or garlic (or both), curry powder, caraway or poppy seeds, dill weed, ground anise, or ground cumin with cottage cheese or sour cream. Let the flavors blend for several hours in the refrigerator before serving.

SPECIFIC POINTERS

▶ Prepare dips or spreads ahead of time, to let the flavors blend and mellow.

▶ Cheeses and cheese dips or spreads should be served at room temperature, so that flavors and aromas are distinct and the texture is perfect.

▶ Serve a variety of crackers—some salted, some plain; some fine-textured, some coarser. Certain cheeses, dips, and spreads are complemented by a plain and simple cracker; some require a stronger-flavored one. Our recipes will provide tips where the choice of cracker is most important.

▶ Raw vegetable pieces are excellent for dipping. Broccoli, cauliflower, and summer squashes are good choices. Crisp vegetables such as carrots, celery, and radishes can be cut into dipping chunks several hours in advance and kept in separate bowls of ice water. Drain and arrange creatively on a platter or in a basket just before serving.

Cheese-Topped Bread

Preparation time: 5 minutes,
      then 2 minutes to broil or bake
Makes: 6 slices

6 slices French bread, or
   3 French buns, sliced in half
2 Tbsp butter
2 Tbsp mayonnaise
1 Tbsp sour cream
2 Tbsp minced onion
1 clove garlic, minced
½ cup grated cheese

Arrange the bread on a baking sheet. In a small saucepan, melt the butter. Stir in the mayonnaise, sour cream, onion, and garlic. When hot, spread on bread. Top with cheese and bake or broil at high heat for 2 minutes to melt cheese and heat through.

Deviled Eggs

Ahead of time: hard-boil and chill the eggs
Preparation time: 10 minutes
Makes: about 8 servings

8 eggs, hard-boiled and chilled
6 Tbsp sour cream
2 tsp Dijon mustard
2 Tbsp minced parsley
1 tsp dill weed
½ tsp olive oil
1 tsp white wine vinegar

Peel the eggs, then slice in half lengthwise. Carefully remove the yolks and place them in a bowl; set whites aside. Mash the yolks with the remaining ingredients. When well blended, fill the cavity of each white with the yolk mixture. Chill until ready to serve.

Tofu Egg Salad

Ahead of time: hard-boil and chill eggs
Preparation time: 10 minutes
Makes: 1½ cups

- 3 Tbsp water
- 1 Tbsp miso
- 5 oz tofu
- 1 Tbsp tahini
- 1 clove garlic, minced
- 1 tsp tamari soy sauce
- 3 hard-boiled eggs, chopped
- 2 Tbsp minced fresh parsley
  Pinch of cayenne pepper (to taste)

Whisk water and miso together in a medium-sized bowl until smooth. Add tofu and tahini and mash together until well combined. Add remaining ingredients and mix well. The mixture should be perfectly smooth and homogeneous.

The longer this sits (up to 2 days), the better it tastes, so if you're going to serve it at a party try to prepare it ahead of time. Tofu egg salad makes a great sandwich spread on whole-grain bread, or can be served as a dip for crackers or fresh vegetables.

All-American Deviled Eggs

Ahead of time: hard-boil and cool the
    eggs
Preparation time: 10 minutes
Makes: 8 servings

- 8 eggs, hard-boiled
- ½ cup mayonnaise
- 2 tsp vinegar
- 2 tsp prepared mustard
  Dash salt
  Dash pepper

Halve the eggs lengthwise and scoop out the yolks carefully. Set the whites aside. Mash the yolks with the mayonnaise, vinegar, mustard, salt, and pepper. Fill the cavities of the egg whites with this mixture. Arrange on a serving dish and chill. Top the eggs with minced parsley or paprika, if desired.

Tofu Avocado Spread

Preparation time: 10 minutes
Makes: 1½ cups

- 1 large, ripe avocado
- 5 oz tofu
- 1 Tbsp lemon juice
- 1 clove garlic, minced
- 2½ tsps prepared hot mustard
- 1 tsp tamari soy sauce
- 2 green onions, thinly sliced
  Dash cayenne pepper

Cut avocado in half, remove pit, and scoop pulp into bowl. Add tofu, broken into chunks. Add remaining ingredients. Mash together, then whip briskly with a fork until well blended.

Serve at once with crisp crackers or vegetables cut into dip-sized chunks, or let flavors blend in the refrigerator. Spread on bread and broil open-face with a slice of cheese to make a delicious sandwich. The spread keeps for a day or two well-covered in the refrigerator, although it will darken as the avocado oxidizes.

Ricotta Avocado Spread

Preparation time: 10 minutes
Makes: 1 cup

- 1 ripe (or slightly overripe) avocado
- ½ cup ricotta cheese
- ⅛ tsp salt
- ½ tsp dill weed
  Freshly ground black pepper to taste
- ⅓ cup finely chopped walnuts

Mash together the first five ingredients until smooth and well blended, then stir in walnuts. Use as a sandwich spread with whole-grain bread and crisp lettuce, or serve as a dip for crackers or fresh vegetables.

Garbanzo Sesame Spread

Preparation time: 10 minutes
Makes: 2 cups

   1   can (15½ oz) garbanzo beans, drained, or
       2 cups freshly cooked garbanzos
  ⅓   cup lemon juice
  ¼   cup tahini
  3   Tbsp chopped green onion
  2   cloves garlic, minced
  ¼   tsp salt
      Parsley (for garnish)

In the blender, combine all ingredients and purée until smooth, thick but spreadable. If the mixture seems too thick, add water or reserved bean liquid. Serve immediately or refrigerate for several days; it tastes better as it ages. Serve with a garnish of fresh parsley. Sesame crackers and fresh vegetables are delicious for dipping.

Garlic Tofu Spread

Preparation time: 10 minutes
Makes: 1 cup

  5   oz tofu
  ⅓   cup olive or sesame oil
3–5   cloves garlic (to taste), minced
  2   tsp miso or 1 Tbsp tamari soy sauce
  2   Tbsp yogurt or buttermilk

Combine all ingredients in a blender or whisk together until thick and smooth. For wonderful garlic bread, spread this mixture on sliced French bread or rolls, sprinkle on a little Parmesan cheese, and bake or broil until the cheese melts.

This spread keeps up to a week in a tightly closed jar in the refrigerator. It can be used as a tasty mayonnaise substitute on sandwiches or vegetables. For the garlic lovers in your life, mix this spread to taste into 1 cup of yogurt, sour cream, or ricotta cheese and use as a dip for vegetables or crackers. When mixed with sour cream, this is delicious with hot steamed artichokes.

Crab Spread

Ahead of time: soften the cream cheese to
 room temperature
Preparation time: 15 minutes
Makes: 1½ cups

8	oz cream cheese, softened
1	Tbsp milk
6½	oz fresh or canned crabmeat
2	Tbsp minced onion
½	tsp prepared horseradish
1	tsp lemon juice
1	clove garlic, minced
1	tsp curry powder

Cream together all ingredients until the mixture is smooth and very well combined. Transfer to a serving bowl or several small pots or ramekins. The flavor improves if allowed to mellow in the refrigerator for several hours, but bring to room temperature again before serving. This spread is a real crowd pleaser. Serve with bread sticks, wholewheat crackers, and fresh vegetables. It is also excellent as a sandwich spread.

Australian Clam Dip

Ahead of time: soften cream cheese to
 room temperature
Preparation time: 10 minutes, plus 1 hour
 to chill
Makes: 2 cups

6	oz canned minced clams
1	lb cream cheese, softened
	Juice of ½ lemon
1	tsp Worcestershire sauce
1–2	cloves garlic, minced

Drain the clams, reserving the liquid. Mix the softened cream cheese with the clam liquid, lemon juice, Worcestershire sauce, and garlic. Beat until smooth. Stir in the clams until well combined. Chill well to blend the flavors. If mixture seems too thick, beat in a little milk before serving.

This dip is excellent with vegetables, crackers, or chips.

Crab-Egg Dip

Ahead of time: hard-boil the eggs, and
    soften butter to room temperature
Preparation time: 15 minutes
Makes: about 2 cups

     ½ cup butter, softened
     2 Tbsp lemon juice
     ½ cup mayonnaise
     ⅓ cup grated Parmesan cheese
     3 hard-boiled egg yolks
  1½ tsp prepared horseradish
     ½ tsp salt
     2 cloves garlic, minced
     ¼ tsp white pepper
     3 hard-boiled egg whites, chopped
     ¼ cup minced onion
     ¼ cup minced parsley
  7½ oz fresh or canned crabmeat *

Whip the butter and lemon juice together
until light and fluffy. Add the mayonnaise
and Parmesan cheese and mix well. Beat in
egg yolks, horseradish, salt, garlic, and pepper. Fold in the remaining ingredients and
mix until well combined. Transfer to a serving dish. Serve chilled with crackers, bread
sticks, and fresh vegetables.

* If using canned crabmeat, rinse and drain
it, and omit the salt.

Hot Crabmeat Dip

Ahead of time: soften cream cheese to
    room temperature
Preparation time: 15 minutes, then 15
    minutes to bake
Makes: 6 servings

     8 oz cream cheese, softened
     1 Tbsp milk
     ½ tsp prepared horseradish
     2 Tbsp minced onion
     1 clove garlic, minced
  6½ oz fresh (or canned) crabmeat
     ⅓ cup sliced toasted almonds*

Preheat oven to 375°. Blend together the
cream cheese, milk, horseradish, onion, and
garlic. When smooth, flake in the crabmeat
and mix well. Spoon into a small casserole
dish or into individual ramekins. Just before
serving, top with toasted almonds, and
bake for 15 minutes. Serve the dip hot with
assorted crackers as an appetizer or a first
course.

* To toast sliced almonds, quickly stir almonds in a hot, cast-iron pan for a couple of
minutes.

Crab Puffs

Preparation time: 15 minutes to assemble,
   then 25 minutes to bake
Makes: 2 to 3 dozen

   ½ lb canned crabmeat, drained and flaked
   ¾ cup grated sharp cheddar cheese
   3 green onions, chopped
   2 cloves garlic, minced
   1 tsp Worcestershire sauce
   1 tsp dry mustard
   1 cup water
   ½ cup butter
   ¼ tsp salt
   1 cup whole wheat pastry flour
   4 eggs
   2 Tbsp white wine

Preheat oven to 400°. In a bowl, combine the crabmeat, cheese, onions, garlic, Worcestershire sauce, and mustard. Blend well and set aside. Combine the water, butter, and salt in a 3-quart saucepan and bring just to a boil. Remove from the heat and immediately whisk in the flour, beating until the mixture leaves the sides of the pan. Add the eggs one at a time, beating thoroughly after each addition. Add the wine and the crab mixture. Blend together thoroughly. Drop by small teaspoonsful onto an ungreased baking sheet. Bake for 15 minutes, then reduce heat to 350° and bake 10 minutes longer or until golden brown. Serve hot.

These crab puffs are delightful served alone or with a dipping sauce such as Creamy Herb Sauce (page 90).

45

Shrimp Spread

Ahead of time: soften cream cheese to
    room temperature
Preparation time: 20 minutes
Makes: 2 cups

    8 oz cream cheese, softened
    ¼ cup sour cream
    ½ tsp chili powder
    1½ tsp cumin
    ½ cup minced onion
    1 cup finely chopped celery
    6 oz fresh shrimp

Blend together the cream cheese, sour
cream, chili powder, and cumin. Stir in the
onion and celery. Mash the shrimp with a
fork and blend into the cheese mixture. If
desired, transfer to a serving bowl or ramekins. Refrigerate until serving time.

This spread is best served with unsalted
crackers, carrot sticks, and cucumber slices.
It should be prepared no more than 6 hours
before serving; if it sits for longer than that,
the water from the celery will ruin the
consistency.

Salmon Log

Ahead of time: soften cream cheese to
    room temperature
Preparation time: 20 minutes, plus 2 hours
    to chill
Makes: one 8 x 2-inch log

    1 lb salmon, canned or baked fresh
    8 oz cream cheese, softened
    2 Tbsp lemon juice
    2 tsp grated onion
    1 tsp prepared horseradish
    ¼ tsp salt
    ½ cup chopped pecans
    ½ cup minced parsley

If using canned salmon, drain it. Flake the
salmon, removing skin and bones. Combine it with the cream cheese, lemon juice,
onion, horseradish, and salt. Mix thoroughly. Chill for at least 2 hours. Combine
the pecans and parsley on a cutting board
or other smooth surface. Shape the salmon
mixture into an 8 x 2-inch log (or two 4 x
2-inch logs), roll it in the nut mixture to coat
all sides evenly, then serve well chilled with
your favorite crackers or rye bread.

Smoked Oyster Roll

Ahead of time: soften cream cheese to
room temperature
Preparation time: 20 minutes, then 30
minutes for chilling
Makes: about 10 servings

    1 tin smoked oysters
    8 oz cream cheese, softened
    1 Tbsp mayonnaise
    1 Tbsp milk
    1 Tbsp lemon juice
    1 clove garlic, minced
    ½ tsp Worcestershire sauce
    ¼ cup minced parsley

Drain the oysters, then mash well with a
fork. Set aside. Cream together the cream
cheese, mayonnaise, milk, lemon juice, garlic, and Worcestershire sauce. Add the
oysters, blending well. Chill this mixture for
about 30 minutes. When firm, roll into a ball
and coat with the parsley. Before serving,
chill for at least a few minutes. This can be
prepared several days ahead if desired;
keep it in the refrigerator, well wrapped.
Serve with crackers or rye bread.

Ginger Dip

Preparation time: 10 minutes, then 45
minutes to chill
Makes: 1 cup

    ½ cup mayonnaise
    ½ cup sour cream
    1 Tbsp minced onion
    2 Tbsp minced parsley
    2 Tbsp finely chopped water chestnuts
    1 Tbsp finely chopped crystallized ginger
    1 clove garlic, minced
    ½ tsp tamari soy sauce

Mix all ingredients together in a bowl until
well blended. Transfer to a serving dish and
chill well. Serve with crackers and crisp
vegetable pieces.

Guacamole (Spicy Avocado Dip)

Preparation time: 15 minutes
Makes: 1½ cups

- 2 avocados, ripe or overripe
- 1 clove garlic, minced
- ¼ cup fresh lemon juice
- 1 tsp tamari soy sauce
- ¼ tsp sea salt
  Cayenne pepper, or
  Minced jalapeño pepper to taste
- 2 Tbsp finely minced or grated onion
- 1 small tomato, finely chopped
- 1 tsp minced cilantro (optional)

Select ripe or just slightly overripe avocados; they will yield to gentle pressure. If you find only hard avocados at your market, bring them home to ripen for a few days in a paper bag or on a window sill where it's easy to remember to check them.

Cut the avocados in half, remove the pits, and scoop the pulp into a bowl. Mash with garlic, lemon juice, tamari soy sauce, salt, and cayenne or minced jalapeño (a pinch of cayenne or ½ teaspoon minced jalapeño will yield a fairly spicy dip). Add the onion, tomato, and cilantro (if used), and stir well. Let flavors blend at room temperature for a few minutes, then chill for at least a few minutes before serving.

Guacamole is perfect with crisp corn chips or fresh vegetable sticks. For a conversation piece, leave one of the avocado pits in the serving bowl—it helps to keep the dip from darkening!

Refreshing Cream Cheese Spread

Ahead of time: soften cream cheese to
    room temperature
Preparation time: 5 minutes
Makes: appetizers for four

  1 tsp capers, undrained
  3 oz cream cheese, softened
  ½ tsp Worcestershire sauce
  ¼ tsp curry powder
  ½ tsp basil

Mash the capers in a small bowl and blend in the cream cheese with a fork. Add the remaining ingredients and blend thoroughly. Transfer to a small serving bowl or ramekin and chill until ready to serve. Serve with crackers, celery sticks, and carrot sticks.

Herb Cheese Ball

Ahead of time: soften cream cheese to
    room temperature
Preparation time: 10 minutes, plus 1 hour
    to chill
Makes: 1 cheese ball

  8 oz cream cheese, softened
  1 clove garlic, minced
  1 tsp caraway seeds
  1 tsp basil
  1 tsp dill weed
  1 tsp chopped chives

Mash the cheese with all other ingredients and blend until smooth. Chill for about an hour, then roll into a ball before serving. Serve on a board, surrounded by a variety of mild-flavored crackers.

Savory Cheese Spread

Ahead of time: soften cream cheese to
    room temperature
Preparation time: 10 minutes, plus 2 hours
    to chill
Makes: 1 cup

    8 oz cream cheese, softened
    1 Tbsp minced parsley
    2 green onions, finely chopped
    1 clove garlic, minced
    1 tsp wine vinegar

Blend all ingredients together until smooth.
Transfer to serving bowl or ramekins and
chill well to blend flavors. Serve at room
temperature. This spread tastes best on a
crisp rye cracker. It will keep in a sealed
container in the refrigerator for up to two
weeks.

Herb Curry Dip

Preparation time: 10 minutes, plus 2 hours
    to chill
Makes: 2 cups

    1 cup cottage cheese
    ½ cup sour cream
    1 tsp basil
    ¼ tsp salt
    ¼–½ tsp curry powder (to taste)
    1 Tbsp minced parsley
    1 Tbsp grated onion
    1½ tsp lemon juice
    ½ tsp Worcestershire sauce
    2 tsp capers, drained

Mix all ingredients together, blending well.
Transfer to a serving dish and chill for two
hours. Serve surrounded by colorful, crisp
vegetables for dipping.

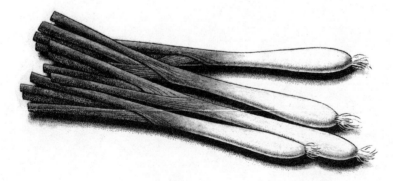

Stuffed Mushrooms

Preparation time: 30 minutes to assemble,
   then 5 minutes to bake
Makes: 12 servings

24 large fresh mushrooms
½ cup grated cheddar cheese
 2 green onions, finely chopped
⅓ cup fine bread crumbs
¼ cup butter, melted
½ tsp salt
½ tsp freshly ground black pepper
½ tsp Italian herb blend (page 31)
½ tsp Worcestershire sauce
 1 clove garlic, minced
   Dash of hot pepper sauce

Preheat oven to 350°. Wash the mushrooms; remove and finely chop the stems. In a medium-sized bowl, combine the chopped stems, cheese, and onion. Add all remaining ingredients except mushroom caps; blend well. Fill mushroom caps with the mixture, mounding slightly in the center. Arrange in a shallow buttered baking dish and bake for 5 minutes. This recipe can be prepared ahead of time, then baked just before serving. Serve on a bed of lettuce, with toothpicks on the side.

Jennifer's Popcorn

Preparation time: 10 minutes
Makes: 2 quarts

 2 qts popped corn (½ cup unpopped)
 2 Tbsp butter
 2 Tbsp brewer's yeast
   Sea salt or tamari soy sauce to taste
   Oregano, garlic, and/or Parmesan cheese
   to taste (optional)

Melt butter in a small pan while you're popping the corn. If you wish, add one teaspoonful of oregano or one minced clove of garlic to the butter as it melts. Toss popped corn with butter and brewer's yeast. Then toss again with a little salt or tamari soy sauce if you wish. Finally, you may add a tablespoonful or two of grated Parmesan cheese.

This popcorn is so delicious, Jennifer often makes a meal of it!

4
SALADS AND DRESSINGS

Salads are a light and refreshing course. Often they are cold and crisp, fresh and seasonal, and delight the palate with their tartness. Salads may be leafy or chunky, or may be simply some fresh vegetable pieces served with a sauce for dipping. Don't limit yourself to traditional concepts about what a salad is or should be. Cooked vegetables, grains, beans, or pasta can provide the inspiration for an unusual salad. A perfect meal for a summer day might consist of two or three very different cold salads, perhaps served with a baguette and a glass of white wine.

Besides being delectable, salads are an important part of our daily fare for practical reasons. Raw fresh vegetables provide roughage, which helps to keep digestion and elimination functioning smoothly. Another nutritional point to consider is that to digest protein-rich foods comfortably, we require hydrochloric acid, so such foods should be eaten on an empty stomach. In other words, vegetable salads, contrary to American custom, should be eaten after your protein course, or all by themselves.

A crucial element in every good salad is its dressing. A salad can be deliciously and instantly dressed by drizzling on a little olive oil, adding some minced fresh or crumbled dry herbs, seasoning lightly with tamari soy sauce, and squeezing a little lemon juice on at the last moment. If you enjoy a more elaborate dressing, by all means take a few minutes to prepare your own once a week. It will keep well in a tightly closed bottle in the refrigerator. Just as convenient to use as the store-bought variety, your homemade dressing will be much more tasty and nutritious.

A good salad with a fresh dressing transcends the ordinary and deserves your special attention in the kitchen.

SPECIFIC POINTERS

▶ You can wash lettuce and other salad greens as soon as they come home from the market. Rinse the head well, drain upside down in a colander for several minutes, then wrap in paper towels and store in the refrigerator crisper drawer in a plastic bag. It will be ready to use when you need it. (If you've acquired a salad spinner, you needn't follow this suggestion, as you have the elite essential that makes washing greens fast and simple.)

▶ Salad-making offers a wonderful opportunity to play with color. If possible, select a variety of brightly colored ingredients and arrange them on the plate to create a salad that looks as good as it tastes.

▶ Almost always, the tartness in a salad dressing can be provided by either lemon juice or vinegar—use them interchangeably.

▶ Nutritionally speaking, virgin olive oil and cold-pressed sesame oil are preferable to most other vegetable oils; superior in flavor as well, these two oils are your best choices for salad dressings.

Ricotta and Fruit Salad

Ahead of time: chill fruit 2—4 hours
Preparation time: 15 minutes
Makes: 6 servings

- ¾ cup ricotta cheese
- ½ cup yogurt
- 1 Tbsp honey
- ½ tsp pure vanilla extract
- 1 tsp ground cinnamon
- 1 large, ripe but firm banana
- 1 medium cantaloupe
- 3 crisp apples

In a bowl, combine the ricotta cheese, yogurt, honey, vanilla, and cinnamon. Blend well and set aside so flavors can blend while you prepare the fruit. Peel and thickly slice the banana. Halve the cantaloupe and scoop out and discard the seeds. Chop the cantaloupe into medium-sized chunks, discarding the peel. Halve and core the apples and cut them into bite-sized chunks. Divide the fruit among serving bowls and arrange the pieces as your whim dictates. Put a large dollop of the dressing on top of each bowl and serve.

Banana-Peanut Fruit Salad

Preparation time: 15 minutes
Makes: 4 to 6 servings

- 2 very ripe bananas
- ½ cup yogurt
- ⅓ cup finely chopped peanuts
- 1 tsp lemon juice
- 2 large oranges
- 2 large, crisp apples

Mash the bananas in a bowl with the yogurt, then stir in the peanuts and lemon juice. Mix well and set aside while you prepare the other fruit. Peel the oranges, divide into sections and cut each section in half, discarding as many seeds as you can. Halve and core the apples and chop into bite-sized chunks. Toss the fruit with the banana dressing. Serve chilled.

Almost Waldorf Salad

Preparation time: 15 minutes
Makes: 4 to 6 servings

- 2   medium crisp apples
- 2   carrots
- ½   lemon
- ⅔   cup ricotta cheese
- ½   cup buttermilk
- 1   tsp molasses
- 1   Tbsp honey
- ½   tsp Chinese 5-spice (page 32)
     or ¼ tsp nutmeg
- ¼   cup raisins
- ¼   cup chopped walnuts
     or sunflower seeds

Core the apples (do not peel) and chop them into bite-sized chunks. Scrub and thinly slice the carrots and combine with apples in a serving bowl; squeeze the juice of ½ lemon over them, toss together, and set aside. In another bowl whisk together the ricotta cheese, buttermilk, molasses, honey, and spices. Stir the nuts (or seeds) and raisins into this mixture. Pour the dressing over the carrots and apples and toss well. Serve immediately, or chill for up to 2 hours and toss again before serving.

Spicy Citrus Salad

Preparation time: 15 minutes
Makes: 6 servings

make ½

- 1½ 3   large navel oranges
- ¼   Half of a small head of green cabbage
- 2   4 Tbsp olive or sesame oil
- ¼ ½   tsp ground cumin
- ¼ ½   tsp ground cardamom
- ⅛ ¼   tsp chili powder
- ⅛ ¼   tsp sea salt
- ¼ ½   tsp honey
- 1   2 Tbsp cider vinegar
- ½   1 avocado, ripe but not overripe
- 2   4 green onions

Peel the oranges, discarding as much white thread-like membrane as possible. Divide the oranges into sections and cut each section in half. Remove the core and finely shred the cabbage. Toss the oranges with the cabbage in a serving bowl. Whisk the oil with the cumin, cardamom, chili powder, and salt, then whisk in the honey and vinegar. Pour this dressing over the oranges and cabbage and toss to coat well. Cut avocado in half, remove pit, and slice avocado into sections. Peel sections and add to orange and cabbage mixture; toss lightly. Trim and finely chop the green onions and sprinkle them over the salad just before serving.

Basic Vegetable Salad

Select one or a few from each of the
following groups of fresh vegetables:
spinach leaves
lettuce leaves

grated cabbage
grated carrots
grated raw beets
sliced tomato
sliced celery
sliced cucumbers
sliced zucchini
sliced mushrooms
fresh peas

grated or sliced onions
chopped green onions
minced fresh garlic
snipped chives
snipped parsley

Select one of the following dried herbs:
tarragon, dill, basil, oregano

Toss your vegetables and herb together in a
bowl and season with a little salt and pepper, olive oil, and lemon juice or vinegar to
taste—or use your favorite dressing.

Spinach Salad

Ahead of time: hard-boil 2 eggs
Preparation time: 20 minutes
Makes: 4 servings

1	bunch fresh spinach
8	mushrooms
2	eggs, hard-boiled
4	tsp sunflower seeds
½	cup mayonnaise
½	cup sour cream
3	Tbsp wine vinegar
¼	tsp sea salt
1–2	cloves garlic, minced
2	thin slices red onion

Carefully wash the spinach and dry the
leaves. Tear the leaves into bite-sized
pieces and arrange on serving plates. Thinly
slice the mushrooms and quarter the eggs.
Arrange these ingredients on the spinach,
then sprinkle the sunflower seeds over all.
In a small bowl, combine the mayonnaise,
sour cream, vinegar, salt, and garlic. Blend
together until creamy. Spoon the dressing
onto the salad, garnishing with several red
onion rings. Serve with whole wheat bread
or crackers.

57

Macaroni Salad

(handwritten: half 4-5)

Ahead of time: hard-boil 4 eggs
Preparation time: 25 minutes
Makes: 8 to 10 servings

(handwritten annotations in left margin: 1/2, 1/2, 2/3, 2, 1, 1, 1, 1/6)

- 1 lb small salad macaroni
- 1 cup chopped cucumber
- ¾ cup minced red onion
- 4 hard-boiled eggs, chopped
- 2 cups mayonnaise
- 2 tsp Dijon mustard
- 1–2 cloves garlic, minced
- ⅓ cup sweet pickles, chopped
  Salt and pepper to taste.

Cook the macaroni in boiling salted water for about 10 minutes or until al dente. (Check package directions and check to see if it is done every minute or so toward the end of the recommended cooking time.) Quickly cool by draining in a colander and rinsing for a few moments with cold water. In a large bowl, combine the well-drained macaroni, cucumber, onion, and eggs. Mix the mayonnaise, mustard, garlic, and pickles in a separate bowl. Pour this dressing over the macaroni and toss well. Salt and pepper to taste. Chill.

Shrimp and Macaroni Salad

Preparation time: 25 minutes
Makes: 6 to 8 servings

- 1 lb small shell macaroni
- 1 cup chopped cucumber
- 1 cup chopped celery
- ¾ cup chopped green onions
- ½ lb small Bay shrimp
- 2 cups mayonnaise
- 1 Tbsp honey
- 1 tsp powdered mustard
- 1 tsp paprika
  Dash of salt and pepper

Cook the macaroni in boiling salted water for about 10 minutes or until al dente. (Check package instructions and check to see if it is done every minute or so toward the end of the recommended cooking time.) Quickly cool by draining in a colander and rinsing for a few moments with cold water. In a large bowl, toss the well-drained macaroni with the cucumber, celery, green onions, and shrimp. In a separate bowl combine the mayonnaise, honey, mustard, paprika, salt, and pepper. Toss the noodle mixture with the dressing and serve.

58

Fettucine Salad with Mushrooms

Preparation time: 20 minutes
Makes: 3 to 4 servings

        2 qts water
        ½ tsp salt
    6–8 large mushrooms
        ½ lb egg noodles
        3 Tbsp olive oil
    1–2 cloves garlic, minced
        2 green onions, thinly sliced
        ½ cup minced parsley
        ½ cup freshly grated Parmesan cheese
        2 tsp fresh lemon juice
        ½ tsp salt
            Cayenne pepper

Bring salted water to a boil in a kettle. Wipe mushrooms clean and slice thinly. Cook noodles in rapidly boiling water for 6—8 minutes or until al dente. Rinse noodles with cold water and drain thoroughly in a colander, then on paper towels, to remove as much water as possible. In a serving bowl toss the noodles with olive oil and minced garlic. Then add remaining ingredients and toss again. The flavor will improve over several hours in the refrigerator, but serve at room temperature. If using long noodles, you may wish to break them into 3-inch lengths before cooking so the salad will be easier to eat.

Celery Seed Cabbage Salad

Preparation time: 15 minutes
Half Makes: 6 servings

    1/4 ½ head of red or green cabbage
    1/2 1 large carrot
        1 2 Tbsp grated onion
    ½ 1 clove garlic, minced
        2 4 Tbsp olive or sesame oil
    1/4 ½ tsp celery seed
            Dash of sea salt
            Dash of black pepper
        1 2 Tbsp fresh lemon juice

Remove the core and finely shred the cabbage. Grate the carrot and toss in a serving bowl with the cabbage. Whisk the onion and garlic in a small bowl with the oil, celery seed, salt, and pepper. Pour this mixture over the salad and toss. Pour on the lemon juice and toss again.

59

Coleslaw

Preparation time: 15 minutes
Makes: 6 servings

- 1 small cabbage, grated
- 3 medium carrots, grated
- 1 cup mayonnaise
- 3 Tbsp wine vinegar
- 2 cloves garlic, minced

In a large bowl, toss together the cabbage and carrots. In a separate bowl, combine the mayonnaise, vinegar, and garlic until perfectly smooth. Pour this over the cabbage mixture and toss well. This salad may be served immediately or may be stored in a tightly covered container in the refrigerator for two or three days.

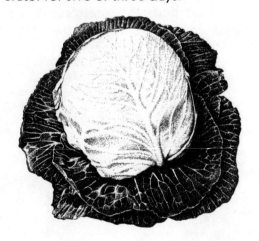

Guy's Curry Vegetable Salad

Preparation time: 15 minutes, then 30
　　　　minutes to chill
Makes: 6 servings

- 2 large carrots, peeled and French-cut
- ½ lb green beans, French-cut into ½-inch pieces
- 2 Tbsp butter
- 1 Tbsp curry powder
- 1 Tbsp prepared mustard
- ¾ cup mayonnaise
- ½ lb firm tofu, cubed

Steam the carrots and beans until al dente, about 7 minutes. Meanwhile, melt the butter in a small saucepan and stir in the curry powder. Add the mustard and mayonnaise. Blend with a wire whisk over low heat until smooth. Combine the steamed vegetables with the tofu and pour the sauce over them. Toss well and chill. Stir before serving.

Potato Salad

Preparation time: 15 minutes to boil
        potatoes, then 15 minutes to prepare
Makes: 6 servings

- 6 potatoes, scrubbed and diced
     (do not peel)
- 1 large cucumber, quartered lengthwise
     and sliced
- 1 large red onion, thinly sliced
- 1 can (3 oz) sliced black olives (optional)
- ¾ cup mayonnaise
- 1 Tbsp plus 1 tsp Dijon mustard
- ½ tsp salt
- ¼ tsp freshly ground black pepper
- 1 Tbsp dill weed

Bring 2 quarts of salted water to a boil in a large pot. Add the potatoes and boil over medium heat for 10 to 15 minutes, until they are just tender but still slightly firm and holding together. Drain in a colander and rinse for just a moment with cold water to stop cooking. Combine well-drained potatoes with the cucumber, onion, and olives in a large bowl and toss well. In a separate bowl combine the mayonnaise, mustard, salt, pepper, and dill weed. Pour this dressing over the potato mixture and toss well. Chill before serving. This potato salad has a wonderful, distinctive flavor!

Peggy's Green Pea Salad

Preparation time: 10 minutes
Makes: 4 to 6 servings

- 2 cups fresh shelled peas or
     thawed, frozen peas
- 1 cup finely chopped celery
- ¼ cup minced onion
- ½ cup chopped, salted peanuts
     or chopped cashews
- 1 clove garlic, minced
- ¼ cup sour cream

Place all ingredients except sour cream in a bowl and toss. Just before serving, add the sour cream, blending in thoroughly. This is a wonderful summer side dish.

Cucumber-Stick Salad

Preparation time: 25 minutes, plus
    chilling time
Makes: 4 servings

  2 medium cucumbers
  1 tsp salt
1–2 Tbsp cider vinegar (to taste)
  2 tsp tamari soy sauce
  1 tsp honey

Peel the cucumbers and halve them lengthwise. Scoop out and discard the seeds and slice the cucumbers into thin sticks. Place them in a colander and sprinkle with the salt. Let stand about 15 minutes, then rinse and drain. Pat dry with a towel to remove any excess water. Put the cucumbers in a bowl and set aside. In a separate bowl, combine the vinegar, tamari, and honey. Pour this over the cucumbers and toss well. Chill before serving.

Sour Cream Cucumbers

Preparation time: 25 minutes, plus
    chilling time
Makes: 4 servings

  1 large cucumber, peeled and thinly
    sliced
  1 tsp salt
  ½ cup sour cream
  4 tsp vinegar
  2 Tbsp chopped chives
  ½ tsp dill weed
    Dash of pepper

Place the cucumber slices in a colander. Sprinkle with the salt and let stand for 15 minutes; rinse and drain. Pat dry with a towel to remove all excess moisture. Combine remaining ingredients in a large bowl, using a whisk to blend thoroughly. Add the cucumbers and toss well to coat them with the sour cream mixture. Chill.

These are a guaranteed hit. Try serving them on red lettuce leaves.

Dill Tomatoes

Preparation time: 10 minutes, then 30
    minutes to chill
Makes: 4 servings

- 4 large, ripe, firm tomatoes
- ¼ cup minced onion
- ½ tsp basil
- ½ tsp dill weed
- 1 Tbsp minced fresh parsley
- 3 Tbsp olive oil
- 2 Tbsp wine vinegar

Slice or quarter the tomatoes. Put them in a bowl with the onion, basil, dill, and parsley. Toss gently to coat the tomatoes with the herbs. Add the oil and vinegar and toss again. Cover and chill for at least 30 minutes before serving.

Arabian Salad

Preparation time: about 15 minutes
Makes: 4 to 6 servings

- 1 cup parsley, minced
- 1 large tomato, cut into wedges
- 1 cup wheat sprouts
- 1 lemon, juiced
- 6–8 fresh mint leaves, finely chopped
- 2 Tbsp olive oil
- ⅛ tsp cinnamon
-    Salt

Mix all ingredients together in a medium-sized bowl. Serve immediately, or chill to blend the flavors further.

Use produce-department wheat sprouts if available, or sprout them yourself. To sprout whole wheat, place 2—3 tablespoons of the grains in the bottom of a quart sprouting jar. Cover with an inch of water and let stand overnight. Next morning drain off the water, rinse and drain again, and lay the jar on its side in a semi-dark place. Rinse and drain morning and evening for 2 to 3 days until wheat sprouts are half-an-inch long. Refrigerate until ready to use.

Bulghur Salad

Preparation time: 25 minutes, plus 30
    minutes for chilling
Makes: 2 to 4 servings

- 1 cup uncooked bulghur wheat
- 2½ cups water
- Salt
- 2 green onions, thinly sliced
- 1 stalk celery, thinly sliced
- 1 cup minced fresh parsley
- 4 Tbsp vinegar
- 1 tsp thyme or marjoram, crumbled

In a medium-sized saucepan combine the bulghur, water, and a little salt. Bring to a boil; cover, reduce heat, and simmer for about 15 minutes or until all the water is absorbed. Combine the bulghur, salt, onions, celery, and parsley in a bowl. Add the vinegar and thyme or marjoram and toss. Chill well. Serve mounded on a bed of lettuce.

Tarragon Tossed Salad

Preparation time: 15 minutes
Makes: 2 servings

- 2 cups fresh salad greens
- 1 Tbsp white wine vinegar
- ¼ tsp dry mustard
- Salt and pepper
- 2 Tbsp olive oil
- 1 Tbsp chopped fresh tarragon, or
  1 tsp dried, crushed tarragon
- 1 Tbsp chopped fresh chervil, or
  1 tsp dried, crushed chervil

Wash and dry the salad greens and tear them into bite-sized pieces. Combine the vinegar, mustard, salt, and pepper in a large salad bowl. Whisk in the oil, then stir in the tarragon and chervil. Add the salad greens and toss well.

This salad is perfect on a hot summer night and is a nice complement to pasta dishes.

Pickled Mushrooms

Preparation time: 15 minutes, plus 2 hours
    to chill
Makes: about 1 quart

- ⅓ cup red wine vinegar
- ⅓ cup olive oil
- 1 small onion, thinly sliced
- 1 tsp salt
- 2 tsp dried parsley or
    2 Tbsp minced fresh parsley
- 1 tsp prepared mustard
- 1 tsp honey
- 1 lb small fresh mushrooms

Combine all ingredients except the mushrooms in a saucepan. Heat over a low flame just to the boiling point. Meanwhile, wash and trim the mushrooms. Add them all at once to the hot marinade; cover and simmer for 5 minutes. Transfer the mushrooms and marinade to a quart jar and let cool to room temperature; then refrigerate for at least 2 hours or up to 2 weeks—the flavor improves with age. To serve, arrange the mushrooms on lettuce leaves. They are a wonderful salad, and also go over well as party appetizers.

Curry Yogurt Dressing

Preparation time: 10 minutes
Makes: 1 cup

- 1 cup plain yogurt
- 2 tsp diced onion
- 1 tsp curry powder
- 1 tsp honey

Put all ingredients in a blender and whir for a moment, or whisk together in a bowl. The honey will dissolve more easily if it is warm. Serve immediately or refrigerate up to a week. An excellent choice for a special salad when the rest of the meal is plain and simple.

Buttermilk Tahini Dressing

Preparation time: 5 minutes
Makes: 1 cup

- ½ cup buttermilk
- ¼ cup tahini
- 1 clove garlic, finely minced
- 2 Tbsp finely minced parsley
- 2 tsp tamari soy sauce
- ½ lemon, juiced

Whisk all ingredients together until smooth. Keeps up to a week in the refrigerator. Try this dressing on a salad that includes tangy greens such as mustard or beet tops.

Blue Cheese Dressing

Preparation time: 10 minutes, plus 30
    minutes to chill
Makes: 2 cups

Half
3|8
1|2 1|6
1|8
1

  ¾ cup crumbled blue cheese
  1 cup mayonnaise
  ⅓ cup sour cream
  ¼ cup wine vinegar
  2 cloves garlic, minced

Using a wooden spoon, mix all ingredients
together in a bowl. The consistency should
be fairly smooth, but allow for some blue
cheese "lumps." Allow flavors to blend for
at least 30 minutes in the refrigerator before
serving. Keeps well for about a week,
refrigerated in a tightly closed container.

Tart Cream Dressing

Preparation time: 5 minutes
Makes: ¾ cup

  ½ cup olive or sesame oil
  2 Tbsp vinegar
  2 Tbsp heavy cream or half-and-half
  ⅛ tsp ground fennel
    Pinch of thyme
  ¼ tsp basil
    Pinch of sage

Blend all ingredients together by whirring in
a blender, shaking vigorously in a small jar
with a tight-fitting lid, or whisking in a bowl.
Serve with your favorite tossed green salad.

French Dressing

Preparation time: 5 minutes
Makes: 1 cup

  ⅔ cup olive oil
  ⅓ cup red wine vinegar
2–3 cloves garlic, minced
  1 Tbsp prepared mustard
  2 Tbsp tomato catsup,
    or tomato juice, or sauce
  1 tsp salt
  1 tsp basil, crushed

Shake all ingredients together in a jar with a
tight-fitting lid. This dressing keeps well in
the refrigerator.

Avocado Dressing

Preparation time: 10 minutes
Makes: 2½ to 3 cups

2	ripe avocados, mashed
½	cup olive oil
¾	cup apple cider vinegar
2–3	cloves garlic, minced
½	lemon, juiced
½	cup mayonnaise
⅛	tsp marjoram
½	tsp ground cumin
⅛	tsp cayenne pepper
1	tsp minced onion

Mix all ingredients together in a bowl until very well blended. This dressing is best served cold, so either chill the bowl and start with your ingredients cold, or make the dressing early and chill before serving. This quantity is perfect for a large gathering; for a smaller amount, reduce all quantities by half. Plan to use the dressing within a day or two, as avocados tend to oxidize rapidly and will darken.

Thousand Island Dressing

Preparation time: 15 minutes
Makes: 1½ cups

½	cup mayonnaise
½	cup yogurt, sour cream, or softened cream cheese
⅓	cup catsup
1–2	cloves garlic, minced
½	tsp salt
¼	tsp pepper
1	tsp prepared salsa
⅛	cup minced sweet pickles
⅓	cup minced onions
⅓	cup minced olives

Mix all ingredients together in a deep bowl, using a wire whisk to blend well. Serve well chilled. This is a great variation of the all-American favorite, especially when it is made with yogurt.

Simple Vinaigrette Dressing

Preparation time: 5 minutes
Makes: ¾ cup

    ½ cup olive oil
    ¼ cup wine vinegar
    1 tsp lemon juice
    ¼ tsp dry mustard
    1 Tbsp chopped parsley
  1–2 cloves garlic, minced

Whisk together the oil, vinegar, lemon juice, and dry mustard until the mixture emulsifies. Then whisk in the parsley and garlic. This dressing can also be made in a blender—just blend at high speed for several seconds. As a variation, omit dry mustard and use either 1 tablespoon Dijon mustard or ¼—½ teaspoon ground anise.

Sesame Tahini Dressing

Preparation time: 5 minutes
Makes: 1 cup

    ½ cup tahini
    ¼ cup olive oil
    ½ lemon, juiced
    ½ cup water
    ½ tsp thyme
    ½ tsp salt
    1 clove garlic, minced

This dressing is most easily made in a blender, although vigorous whisking will do the trick. Blend all ingredients together until smooth. Chill before serving. Keeps well in the refrigerator for up to two weeks.

Cocktail Sauce

Preparation time: 5 minutes
Makes: ⅔ cup

    ½ cup catsup
  2–3 Tbsp lemon juice
    1 clove garlic, minced
    2 tsp Worcestershire sauce
    ½ tsp grated onion or
      dry onion flakes
    1 tsp horseradish (or more to taste)

Whisk all ingredients together, blending well. Serve well chilled. If you wish to serve immediately, mix in a well-chilled bowl. This dressing will stay fresh for up to a week, stored, tightly covered, in the refrigerator.

Mustard Sesame Dressing

Preparation time: 5 minutes
Makes: ¾ cup

- ⅓ cup sesame oil
- 3 Tbsp tahini
- 1 Tbsp mayonnaise
- 1 small clove garlic, minced
  Pinch of salt
- 1 tsp Dijon mustard
- 2 Tbsp red wine vinegar

Whisk all ingredients together until smooth, or whir in a blender. This rich dressing is especially good on leftover grain or legume salads, and is also wonderful as a sauce over hot or cold cooked broccoli, cauliflower, cabbage, or brussels sprouts.

Dill Sesame Dressing

Preparation time: 5 minutes
Makes: 1 cup

- ⅓ cup sesame oil
- 2 Tbsp tahini
- 1 large clove garlic, minced
- 1 tsp tamari soy sauce
- 1 tsp dill weed
- 2 tsp Dijon mustard
  Juice of 1 lemon (about ¼ cup)
- 1 Tbsp water

Whisk all ingredients together, or shake vigorously in a tightly covered bottle or jar, until absolutely smooth. Keeps for up to 2 weeks, if tightly covered, in the refrigerator. Shake well or whisk again before each use.

5

SOUPS

There is a commonly quoted myth that good soups have to simmer on the stove for hours. Some soups, however, are simple to prepare, yet offer as much flavor, aroma and satisfaction as their time-consuming cousins.

Soup can serve as the hearty focus of attention for a meal, perhaps accompanied by bread or rolls and a green salad. On the other hand, a light and delicate soup serves well as a non-filling first course, stimulating the appetite for what's to come.

We offer here some of our favorite recipes and encourage you to invent your own soups by experimenting with a free hand, tasting as you go.

SPECIFIC POINTERS

▶ Acquire a heavy pot of at least a 4-quart capacity, with a lid. It will serve you well for many purposes in addition to soup-making (steaming artichokes, boiling noodles, etc.).

▶ If you want the distinct flavor of each vegetable in a soup to come through, don't put everything in the pot at once. Start the broth with whatever requires the most cooking, then add the more delicate vegetables in the appropriate order so that each one is just tender when the soup is done.

▶ Most soups, with the possible exception of cream-based ones, can be frozen. Any soup can be stored, tightly covered, in the refrigerator for a few days. Some soups even improve in the process! Reheat soups gently.

▶ Almost anything can be made into soup. "Odds-and-ends soup" is what you make when you think there's nothing to fix for dinner. Small amounts of vegetables, cooked grains, tofu, and leftovers can be cooked in water with whatever flavorings you choose. Just keep adding seasonings, a little at a time, until you think it tastes good!

▶ To save yourself and friends from scorched taste buds, allow soup to cool for a few minutes before serving.

Broths

You needn't depend on bouillon cubes or meat juices for a rich soup broth. Here are some quick and much more nutritious ways to the same end:

Miso is a high-protein savory soybean paste that is added to hot soup just before serving (about 1 tablespoon to 1 quart of soup). Whisk it with a few tablespoons of water, then stir into hot soup.

Marmite™ is a brewer's-yeast extract flavored with vegetables and spices. It is dissolved in hot water (1 teaspoon to 2 cups) and serves as the soup's beginning broth.

Vegetable broth powder or cubes are made of powdered dried vegetables and spices. They are dissolved in hot water like meat-flavored bouillon (1 teaspoon or 1 cube to 1 cup).

Eggplant and Fresh Basil Soup

Preparation time: 40 minutes
Makes: 4 to 6 servings

    5 cups water
    2 medium eggplants (about 1½ lbs)
    1 small bell pepper
    1 tsp salt
       Minced garlic, 3 cloves or more
    ⅔ cup fresh basil leaves, minced
    ½ cup half-and-half
    ½ cup freshly grated Parmesan cheese
    2 eggs

Bring water to a boil in a large pot. Peel one of the eggplants and wash the other. Cube them both. Halve and sliver the bell pepper. Put the eggplant and bell pepper in the boiling water with salt and boil for 10 minutes. Remove from heat, cover, and let stand for about 20 minutes. Return the soup to a simmer and add the garlic and basil. Simmer for 3 minutes. Beat the eggs in a small bowl. Just before serving, remove the soup from heat and add the half-and-half, cheese, and eggs. Stir and serve.

Carrot Curry Soup

Preparation time: 45 minutes
Makes: 2 to 4 servings*

    2 Tbsp butter
    1 medium onion, chopped
    1 large carrot, thinly sliced
    1 tsp curry powder
    3 cups broth or water
    ⅓ cup bulghur wheat, uncooked
    ½ tsp salt
    ¼ tsp pepper
    ½ cup plain yogurt
    ⅓ cup half-and-half
       Fresh parsley, minced (for garnish)

Melt butter in a 3-quart saucepan; add the onion and carrot. Cover and cook over low heat about 10 minutes. Stir in curry powder, broth, bulghur wheat, salt, and pepper. Bring to a boil; reduce heat and cook, covered, for about 20 minutes. Remove from heat, pour (or ladle) into blender jar, and purée. This may have to be done in several batches. Return to pan, stir in the yogurt and half-and-half. Reheat and serve with a minced fresh parsley garnish—it really tops off the flavor.

* This is a good first course for a curry dinner for four people. As a "main course" for four, double the amounts.

Tomato Soup

Preparation time: 45 minutes
Makes: 4 to 6 servings

- 1 can (16 oz) tomatoes
- 5 cups water
- 1 small can (3½ oz) tomato paste
- 4 potatoes, peeled and finely chopped
- 1 onion, chopped
- ½ tsp salt
- 1 tsp dill weed
- 4 cloves garlic, minced
- 1 tsp dried basil
- ½ tsp dried oregano
  pinch of cayenne pepper
- 2 Tbsp butter
- ½ cup sour cream
  Grated Parmesan cheese (optional)

Chop the canned tomatoes. Put all ingredients except the butter and sour cream into a large pot and bring to a boil. Reduce heat and simmer for 30 minutes or until potatoes are tender. Remove from heat and blend in butter and sour cream. Serve piping hot, sprinkled with grated Parmesan cheese if desired.

New England Clam Chowder

Preparation time: 30 minutes
Makes: 2 generous servings

- 2 Tbsp butter
- ¼ cup minced onion
- 1 can (14 oz) minced clams, or
  1 pint fresh clams, minced
- 2 cups diced potatoes
- ½ cup water
- 1 cup half-and-half
- 1 tsp salt
- ⅛ tsp pepper
- 1 Tbsp whole wheat pastry flour, or
  ½ tsp arrowroot powder (optional)

Melt the butter in a large pot. Add the onion and sauté until tender. Drain the liquid off the clams into the soup pot, then add the potatoes and water. Simmer until potatoes are tender, about 15 minutes. Add the clams, half-and-half, salt, and pepper. Heat through. If desired, thicken with flour or arrowroot powder (ladle a small amount of the hot soup liquid into a jar with a tight-fitting lid, and add the flour or arrowroot powder; cover tightly and shake to dissolve; then return to the soup pot and stir until thick).

This soup is delicious with soda crackers and butter.

Tortilla Soup

Preparation time: 30 minutes
Makes: 6 to 8 servings

    4 cups water
    3 cloves garlic, minced
    1 large red onion, sliced
    1 tsp salt
    ⅛ tsp freshly ground black pepper
    8 oz fresh mushrooms
      Oil for deep-frying tortillas
    6 corn tortillas
  1½ cups tomato purée
    1 cup half-and-half
    ¼ cup prepared salsa
    2 tsp minced fresh cilantro (optional)
    ½ cups freshly grated Parmesan cheese

Put the water, garlic, onion, salt, and black pepper in a kettle over medium heat. Wipe the mushrooms clean and slice them thickly, then add them to the kettle. Reduce heat and simmer for 10 minutes. Meanwhile, pour oil in a saucepan to a depth of about 1½ inches and heat over a medium flame. Cut the tortillas into eighths and fry them in the hot oil, one layer at a time, until crisp. (To make sure oil is hot enough, drop one strip in—if it sizzles immediately, the oil is ready. If the oil begins to smoke, remove pan from heat, reduce heat slightly and return the pan to the burner when smoking ceases.) When mushroom broth is done, stir in the tomato purée, half-and-half, salsa, and cilantro, and simmer for 5 minutes longer. Divide tortilla chips among serving bowls and top with some grated Parmesan—or let your guests do this. Ladle hot soup into the bowls at the table.

It is important in this recipe to use unsalted "real" tortilla chips. If you do not want to fry your own, buy a bagful from a Mexican restaurant that makes its own chips daily.

Fish Stew

Preparation time: 45 minutes
Makes: 2 to 4 servings

- 4 Tbsp butter
- 2 Tbsp olive oil
- 2 stalks celery, sliced
- 3 cloves garlic, minced
- ¼ cup diced onion
- 1 qt tomato juice
- 1 potato, cubed
- 8 oz cod or red snapper fillets, cut into chunks
- 1 tsp basil
- 2 Tbsp dried parsley
- 2 Tbsp tamari soy sauce
- ½ cup white wine
- 1 tsp salt
   Freshly ground black pepper

Heat the butter and oil in a large saucepan. Sauté the celery, garlic, and onion for several minutes. Add all remaining ingredients and bring to a boil. Reduce heat and simmer for 35 minutes. Add a bit of water while cooking if the broth is greatly reduced. Serve with hot French bread and wine.

Cheese Soup

Preparation time: 25 minutes
Makes: 4 to 6 servings

- ½ small onion, minced
- 4 cups milk
- 3 Tbsp butter
- 3 Tbsp whole wheat pastry flour
- 1½ cups grated cheddar cheese
- ½ tsp sea salt
- ½ tsp paprika
- 2 Tbsp minced parsley
- 3 slices bread

Put the onion and milk in a saucepan and bring almost to a boil. Remove from heat. Meanwhile, melt the butter in a soup pot, then add the flour and stir for a minute or two over low heat before whisking in the milk. Cook over low heat, stirring frequently, until mixture thickens and comes to a slow boil. Remove from heat, then add the cheese, salt, paprika, and parsley, and stir until cheese melts and is smoothly incorporated into soup. Meanwhile, toast bread, cut each slice into 4 triangles, and put 2 or 3 triangles in the bottom of each bowl. Pour the hot soup over them and serve.

Corn Chowder

Preparation time: 25 minutes
Makes: 4 to 6 servings

    4 cups corn, fresh or frozen
    2 medium potatoes, chopped
    1 small onion, thinly sliced
    2 cups broth
    1 cup water
    2 cups hot milk
    ½ tsp salt
    ⅛ tsp pepper
    1 Tbsp butter
       Minced parsley (for garnish)

In a large saucepan combine the corn, potatoes, onion, broth, and water. Bring to a boil; reduce heat and simmer for 15 minutes. Remove from heat and add the milk, salt, pepper, and butter. One cup at a time, place in a blender jar and purée. Keep hot, if necessary, in a double boiler. Top with minced parsley and serve with whole wheat bread.

Zucchini and Pea Soup

Preparation time: 25 minutes
Makes: 2 servings

    1½ cups broth or water
    1   medium zucchini, thinly sliced
    ½   cup fresh or frozen green peas
    ¼   cup chopped onion
    ½   tsp dried chervil
    1   Tbsp butter
        Dash of salt
        Freshly ground black pepper

Combine the broth, zucchini, peas, onion, and chervil in a saucepan. Bring to a boil over medium heat; reduce heat and simmer for 10 minutes. Purée in a blender until smooth, then return to pot and warm over low heat. Whisk in the butter, and season to taste with salt and freshly ground black pepper.

Spinach Soup with Lemon

Ahead of time: cook ½ cup rice, or
      bulghur (yield: 1 cup cooked)
Preparation time: 30 minutes
Makes: 4 servings

  2 bunches spinach
  2 Tbsp oil
  4 cups water
  ½ cup chopped onion
½ – ¾ cup milk
  1 tsp curry powder
  ½ tsp salt
  1 cup cooked rice or bulghur
  1 lemon, cut into wedges

Wash the spinach carefully (discarding stems), and chop leaves. Heat the oil in a large pot and sauté the onion until translucent. Add the water and spincach and bring almost to a boil. When spinach is wilted and soup is hot, add the milk, curry powder, salt, and rice or bulghur. Heat through and serve immediately with wedges of lemon that are to be squeezed into soup.

Potato Soup

Preparation time: 35 to 40 minutes
Makes: 4 to 6 servings

 3½ cups water
  5 large russet potatoes, scrubbed
    and diced (do not peel)
3–4 leeks, chopped
 1½ cups milk
  ½ tsp caraway seeds, toasted
  2 Tbsp dill weed
  1 tsp salt
    Freshly ground black pepper
  ½ cup sour cream
  4 Tbsp butter

Heat the water; add the potatoes and leeks and cook over medium heat for 20 minutes or until potatoes are just tender. Add the milk, caraway seeds, dill, salt, and pepper. Simmer for 15 to 20 minutes until fairly thick. If necessary, mash some of the potatoes against the side of the pot to thicken the soup. Just before serving, stir in the sour cream and butter.

This is a wonderful soup! Its great served with hot French bread or whole-grain rolls and a hearty red wine.

Zucchini Chowder

Preparation time: 40 minutes
Makes: 8 servings

(handwritten: 4sew)

1½	3 qts water
1½	3 cups thinly sliced zucchini
½	1 large onion
½	1 bell pepper
½	1 tsp curry powder
2	4 tsp tamari soy sauce
½	1 clove garlic, minced
	½ tsp salt
	1 cup leftover cooked grains or
	½ cup dry bulghur or millet
	1 Tbsp miso
	1 egg
	2 Tbsp chopped parsley
	Cayenne pepper to taste

Put 3 quarts of water to boil in a large kettle. If you are using a very large zucchini, cut it lengthwise into fourths or sixths, before cutting each section into thin slices. Halve the onion lengthwise and slice each half thinly. Halve the bell pepper, discard the seeds and inner membrane, then slice into thin shreds. Put the zucchini, onion, and bell pepper into the heating water along with the curry powder, tamari, garlic, salt, and the cooked or dry grains. When this mixture comes to a boil, lower the heat and simmer for 20 minutes. Meanwhile whisk the miso into the egg in a small bowl. When cooking time is up, remove the soup from heat and add the miso/egg mixture, parsley, and cayenne. Let it sit for a few moments before stirring to disperse the egg. Now serve very hot. This recipe is perfect for that gigantic zucchini from your (or your neighbor's) garden!

Vegetable Miso Soup

Preparation time: 25 minutes
Makes: 4 to 6 servings

    2 qts water
    1 large onion, diced or sliced
    2 cloves garlic, minced
    ¼ tsp salt
    1 large potato, scrubbed and diced small
    ½ cup uncooked bulghur wheat
    2 cups uniformly chopped broccoli
    2 cups uniformly sliced zucchini
      or other summer squash
    1 cup (packed) washed and torn greens
    1 Tbsp miso
    1 egg
    1 tsp tamari soy sauce
      Cayenne pepper to taste

Heat the water to boiling in a large kettle while you prepare the vegetables. Add the onion, garlic, salt, potato, and bulghur wheat to the hot water and cook over medium heat for about 8 minutes. Add the broccoli and cook 5 minutes longer. Add the zucchini and cook 5 minutes longer. Add the greens and stir until they wilt. Remove from heat. Whisk the miso with egg in a small bowl. Add the tamari and miso/

egg mixture to the soup with a little cayenne pepper and let stand for a few moments before stirring to disperse the egg and blend in miso.

This hearty soup requires no accompaniment, except perhaps a thick slice of whole-grain bread.

Broccoli Soup
with Cheese and Ginger

Preparation time: 40 minutes
Makes: 4 to 6 servings

- 6 cups water
- 3 cups finely chopped broccoli
- 1 large onion, chopped
- 3 cloves garlic, minced
- 1 Tbsp tamari soy sauce
- 2 tsp grated fresh ginger root
- ¼ cup pine nuts (optional)
  or chopped walnuts (optional)
  Dash of cayenne
- 1 Tbsp miso, whisked to a paste with 2 Tbsp water
- 1 cup grated cheddar cheese

Bring the water to a boil in a large pot, then add the broccoli, onion, and garlic. When water returns to a boil, reduce heat and simmer for 15 to 20 minutes, or until broccoli is very tender. Press through a sieve or purée in a blender until smooth, then return to the pot and add the tamari, ginger root, and nuts. Stir over low heat for about 5 minutes. Turn off the heat; add the cayenne, miso, and cheese, and stir until cheese melts and incorporates perfectly into the soup. Serve at once.

With cornbread and a light salad, this soup makes a hearty and delicious meal.

Cream of Broccoli Soup

Preparation time: 20 minutes
Makes: 3 to 4 servings

- 4 cups chopped broccoli (about 2 heads)
- 1½ cups water
- 3 cups milk
- 6 Tbsp butter
- ½ tsp thyme
- 6 Tbsp whole wheat pastry flour
- 1 bay leaf
- ½ tsp salt
- ¼ tsp black pepper
- 2 tsp sherry (optional)

Put the broccoli in a pan with the water, cover and bring to a boil. Reduce heat and simmer until just tender, 7—10 minutes. Meanwhile, gently heat the milk; keep warm but do not boil. In a separate large pot, make a roux by melting the butter with the thyme and stirring in the flour. Stir and cook for a moment over low heat, then slowly add the warmed milk, then the salt, pepper, and bay leaf. Whisk until smooth and thickened. Now stir in the hot cooked broccoli along with its cooking liquid, and the sherry. Stir for a few more minutes, then serve.

Guy's 20-Minute Vegetable Stew

Preparation time: 35 minutes
Makes: 8 servings

- ¼ cup butter
- 1 large onion, chopped

- 1 heart and stalk section of a small cauliflower, chopped
- 3 stalks broccoli, chopped
- 1 potato, chopped
- 5 cloves garlic, minced
- 1 can (14 oz) stewed tomatoes
- 2 Tbsp Italian seasoning (page 31)

  Flowerets of a small cauliflower
  Flowerets of 3 stalks of broccoli
- 2 potatoes, diced
- ¼ cup tamari soy sauce
- 3 bay leaves
- 1 tsp lemon pepper
- 2 Tbsp vinegar

Melt the butter in a large soup pot and sauté the onion over low heat. Meanwhile, place the chopped cauliflower heart, broccoli stalks, chopped potato, garlic, stewed tomatoes, and Italian seasoning in a blender and purée. You may need to do this in two batches. Add enough water each time just to cover the vegetables. This thick vegetable base should be added directly to the sautéed onion. Heat through over medium heat. Add the broccoli and cauliflower flowerets, the diced potatoes, tamari, bay leaves, pepper, and vinegar. Cook for 20 minutes until the vegetables are tender. If the stew is too thick, add a bit of water. Serve piping hot with whole wheat bread or rolls.

6

SAUCES

There's a mystique surrounding sauces, perhaps because many fine restaurants hire a trained chef exclusively for sauce-making. Indeed, some sauces do require hours of careful attention. There is, however, a vast array of wonderful sauces that are quick and easy to prepare. The very simplest need not even be cooked. Butter and herbs tossed with hot steamed vegetables or noodles make an instant sauce. Taking a little more time, you can whip together a cheese sauce or Hollandaise that will steal the show at mealtime.

If you want to include a sauce, plan a fairly light meal. For instance, select a simple vegetable recipe, without a sauce, and a simply dressed salad to accompany a sauced pasta. Too many sauces served together may compete in flavor and will leave the diner feeling heavy and sluggish.

You can try our foolproof sauce recipes with confidence, even if sauce-making is unfamiliar to you. Once you've mastered a few very simple techniques, you'll have a repertoire of sauces to draw upon that can transform any meal into a gourmet delight at a moment's notice.

Thickening Agents

There are a number of substances that can be used to thicken a liquid into a sauce or gel. Since we cannot recommend white flour, gelatin, or cornstarch (all highly processed foods), we provide here formulas for more healthful substitutes.

For white flour, substitute:
Equal amount of whole wheat pastry flour, or
50% more regular whole wheat flour, or
50% more powdered arrowroot

For gelatin, substitute:
1 Tbsp agar-agar flakes to gel 2 cups liquid to the soft stage, or
2 Tbsp agar-agar flakes to gel 3½ cups liquid to the firm stage

For cornstarch, substitute:
Twice as much whole wheat pastry flour, or
Three times as much regular whole wheat flour, or
Three times as much powdered arrowroot

Agar-agar is a seaweed derivative used in place of animal gelatin in molded salads or desserts. It gels readily at room temperature, and a little goes a long way. To gel 3½ cups liquid to the firm stage, use 2 tablespoons agar-agar flakes, or 1 tablespoon granulated agar-agar, or 1¼ agar-agar sticks.

Powdered arrowroot is the ground rootstock of a tropical American plant. It is an unrefined product high in minerals (particularly calcium) and is easily digestible. It thickens when heated with liquid, yielding a very smooth sauce. To use, dissolve powdered arrowroot in a small amount of your cooking liquid or in water before adding to the recipe. Arrowroot will create a gummy texture if cooked too long, so add it toward the end of the cooking time and continue cooking only long enough to thicken and heat through. To thicken 1 cup of liquid, use 1½ tablespoons powdered arrowroot.

SPECIFIC POINTERS

▶ Using a wire whisk to stir sauces as they cook saves time and prevents frustrating lumps.

▶ Sauces must be cooked at a low temperature and should be stirred frequently to avoid scorching.

▶ A flour-thickened sauce begins with a roux. Melt butter in a pan and gently stir in an equal amount of flour. Let this roux cook for a moment or two over very low heat before adding preheated liquid. Whisk, or stir frequently, until the sauce thickens.

▶ If an egg is used to help thicken a sauce, stir it with a bit of the hot liquid in a bowl, then add to the sauce in a thin stream, stirring all the while. Watch the temperature closely, as boiling will curdle an egg-thickened sauce.

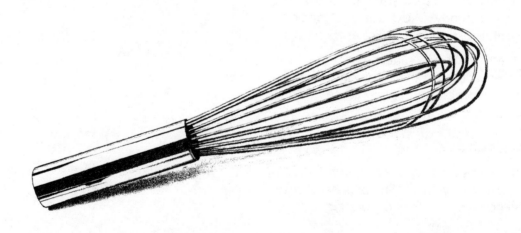

Basic White Sauce

Preparation time: 20 minutes
Makes: 1 cup

    1 Tbsp butter
    4 tsp whole wheat pastry flour
    1 cup milk, heated
       Pinch of salt
       Dash of pepper (white, black, or
       cayenne)

Heat milk in a saucepan until warm (not hot). Meanwhile, melt butter in a separate saucepan, then add flour and stir over very low heat for a minute or two. Now pour in the hot milk in a steady stream, whisking or stirring constantly. Add salt and pepper and continue stirring until thick and smooth.

Many different sauces can be made from this recipe by the addition of herbs, spices, or other flavorings. Some of our favorite variations are:

Cheese Sauce

When the Basic White Sauce is done, add ½ to 1 cup grated cheese. Stir until the cheese melts and is smoothly incorporated.

Curry Sauce

Alter the Basic White Sauce recipe by adding 1 teaspoon curry powder (or a little more or less, according to taste) to the butter before adding the flour, then proceed as in basic recipe.

Wine Sauce

Make the Basic White Sauce then whisk in 1 tablespoonful white wine or sherry just before serving.

Serve these sauces on vegetables, grains, or fish and you've created a gourmet meal almost instantly!

Bordelaise Sauce

Preparation time: 30 minutes
Makes: 2¼ cups

    ¾ cup finely chopped fresh mushrooms
    1 Tbsp butter
    3 Tbsp cornstarch (do not substitute)*
    2 cups stock
    2 tsp dried tarragon, crushed
    2 Tbsp lemon juice
    3 Tbsp red wine

Sauté the mushroom pieces in butter until tender. Mix the cornstarch with ¼ cup of the cool stock in a jar. Shake well to dissolve, then stir in with the mushrooms, adding the rest of the stock. Reduce heat, add the tarragon, lemon juice, and wine. Simmer 5 to 10 minutes, stirring frequently. This sauce has the consistency of a reduced sauce rather than a very thick sauce. Though not as quick as some, this sauce is easy, and if started before beginning the meal preparation it will be done at just the right moment. It is a delicious topping for broiled fish, steamed vegetables, or noodles.

* Do not substitute arrowroot powder in this recipe: the prolonged cooking time would make a gummy sauce.

Wine Mushroom Sauce

Preparation time: 20 minutes
Makes: 1½ cups

    1 cup sliced fresh mushrooms
    ¼ cup finely chopped green onion
    ¼ cup butter
    4 tsp arrowroot powder
    2 Tbsp minced parsley
       Dash of salt and pepper
    ¾ cup red or white wine
    ¾ cup water

Sauté the mushrooms and onions in the butter over medium heat, stirring frequently, until the mushrooms have released their liquid. Immediately add the water and salt and pepper. Heat to a simmer; add parsley. Meanwhile, blend the arrowroot powder with the wine in a jar with a tight-fitting lid; shake well to dissolve. Add the arrowroot liquid to the hot sauce. Cook and stir until thick and bubbly. Serve very hot over cooked grains or your favorite pasta.

Dijon Sour Cream Sauce

Preparation time: 10 minutes
Makes: ⅔ cup

- 1 tsp butter
- ½ cup sour cream
- 1 tsp Dijon mustard
- 1 Tbsp white wine or lemon juice

Melt the butter in a saucepan over low heat. Whisk in the sour cream, mustard, and wine. Heat slowly until hot, stirring frequently. This sauce is wonderful over poached eggs, steamed vegetables, or noodles.

Creamy Herb Sauce

Preparation time: 5 minutes
Makes: 1 cup

- ½ cup mayonnaise
- ½ cup sour cream
- 1 tsp dill weed, or tarragon, or dried basil
- 1 small clove garlic, minced (optional)

Combine all ingredients well and chill as long as possible before serving, to allow flavors to blend. Serve at room temperature over your favorite hot or cold vegetable or as a vegetable dipping sauce (try it with artichokes!).

Miso Tahini Sauce

Preparation time: 5 minutes
Makes: ¾ cup

- 1 Tbsp miso
- 4 Tbsp tahini
- ¼ cup water
  Juice of ½ lemon (about 2 Tbsp)
- 1 small clove garlic, minced (optional)

Whisk all ingredients together. Serve cold, or at room temperature, or stir over low heat until hot. This rich and delicious sauce enhances hot or cold steamed vegetables or grains and is a great protein-booster.

90

Dill Horseradish Sauce

Preparation time: 5 minutes
Makes: 2 cups (6—8 servings)

1 pint sour cream
2 Tbsp prepared horseradish
1 tsp dill weed
1–2 Tbsp white wine

Whisk all ingredients together. Serve cold, or heat slowly in a small saucepan until almost boiling. You may serve immediately over hot vegetables or refrigerate in a covered container for future use as a sauce or dip. It will stay fresh for up to 2 weeks.

Mint Sauce

Preparation time: 10 minutes, then
30 minutes for steeping
Makes: ½ cup

½ cup vinegar
¼ cup water
2 Tbsp honey
Dash salt
½ cup finely minced fresh mint leaves

Combine the vinegar, water, honey, and salt in a small saucepan. Bring just to a boil, reduce heat, and simmer uncovered for 5 minutes. Pour over the mint leaves in a bowl and let steep for 30 minutes. Strain the liquid, and discard most of the mint. Serve hot or cold.

This traditional English mint sauce, liquidy rather than thick, is especially good served over boiled new potatoes.

Quick Rarebit Sauce

Preparation time: 15 minutes
Makes: 1½ cups

- ¾ cup cultured buttermilk
- 1½ cups grated cheddar cheese
- 1 Tbsp miso
- 1½ tsp prepared spicy mustard

Whisk all ingredients together in a saucepan and heat slowly, whisking occasionally, until cheese melts—about 10 minutes. Serve over eggs and toast or grains.

Teriyaki Sauce

Preparation time: 5 minutes
Makes: 4—6 servings

- ⅓ cup tamari soy sauce
- 2 Tbsp dry sherry
- 1 Tbsp molasses
- ¼ tsp ground ginger
- 2 cloves garlic, minced

Whisk all ingredients together. This sauce may be used as a dipping sauce or as a marinade for fish, tofu, or vegetables.

Hollandaise Sauce

Special requirement: a blender
Preparation time: 5 minutes
Makes: 1 cup

- 3 egg yolks
- 2 Tbsp lemon juice
  Dash cayenne pepper
- 4 oz butter

Place the egg yolks, lemon juice, and cayenne in the blender container. Cover and quickly turn blender off and on for several seconds. Meanwhile, heat the butter until melted and almost bubbling. Turn blender on high speed, and slowly pour in the butter. Blend until thick and fluffy, about 30 seconds. If not serving immediately, keep warm in a double boiler. Try this sauce over any fresh vegetable; it's also good over noodles or eggs.

This is an easy Hollandaise. Since the preparation time is minimal, we suggest making it just before serving.

Mayonnaise

Special requirement: a blender
Preparation time: 15 minutes
Makes: about 1½ cups

    1 egg
    1 tsp salt
    1 tsp powdered mustard
    1 cup olive oil*
    1 Tbsp lemon juice
    2 Tbsp wine vinegar

Mix the egg, salt, mustard, and ¼ cup oil in the blender for a few seconds. With blender still on, slowly add ½ cup more oil in a thin, steady stream. Then add the lemon juice and blend well. Continue blending while adding the remaining oil and the vinegar.

* You may use any vegetable oil for this recipe, but a fruity, virgin olive oil will yield the finest flavor.

Honey Mayonnaise

Preparation time: 5 minutes
Makes: 2 cups

    2 cups mayonnaise
    1 Tbsp honey
    1 tsp ground mustard
    1 tsp paprika
       Dash salt and pepper

Mix all ingredients together until well blended. This sauce is good hot over vegetables (you may want to halve the recipe for this) or cold on pasta salads.

Tofu Sesame Sauce

Special requirement: a blender
Preparation time: 10 minutes
Makes: 1½ cups

    12 oz tofu
    ¼ cup tahini
    1 Tbsp tamari soy sauce
    1 Tbsp honey

Drain fresh tofu and press between paper towels to remove as much water as possible. Combine all ingredients in a blender and blend until perfectly smooth. Serve over hot or cold vegetables.

Salsa

Preparation time: 15 minutes, then 2—4
    hours for flavors to blend
Makes: 2 cups

  6 fresh, ripe tomatoes
  1 small onion, finely chopped or grated
  1 clove garlic, minced
  2 Tbsp canned green chiles, minced or
    1 small fresh jalapeño pepper, seeded
    and finely minced
¼ tsp salt
  1 Tbsp minced fresh cilantro or
    1 tsp dried cilantro (optional)

Finely chop the tomatoes, discarding stem ends and saving any juice that runs off. Add the onion and garlic to the tomatoes and their juice. Stir in the chiles, salt, and cilantro. If using a fresh jalapeño, be sure to wear gloves: the juice from these peppers can burn you painfully. Let the salsa sit in the refrigerator for a few hours or up to a week. Serve at room temperature as a dip for corn chips or as a condiment.

Tomato Sauce

Preparation time: 35 minutes
Makes: about 4 cups

¼ cup olive oil
  2 cloves garlic, minced
  1 medium onion, minced
  1 bell pepper, chopped
  1 Tbsp dried basil
  3 lbs fresh tomatoes, chopped or
    2 cans (28 oz each) whole tomatoes,
    chopped
  1 large bay leaf
  1 can (3 oz) chopped or sliced black
    olives
  2 thin lemon slices
½ cup red or white wine

Heat the olive oil in a large pan. Add the garlic and onion and sauté until tender over low heat. Add the bell pepper and sauté 3 minutes longer. Crumble in the basil, and add the tomatoes, bay leaf, and olives. Bring to a boil, stirring several times. Reduce heat to a simmer and add the lemon slices and wine. Simmer for at least 20 minutes or as long as 1 hour. Be sure to stir occasionally. This sauce is wonderful over spaghetti or in manicotti or lasagna. To use as a spaghetti sauce, cook from 45 minutes to an hour for a good thick sauce.

SAUCES

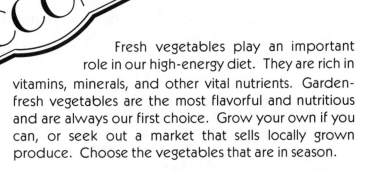

7

VEGETABLE ACCOMPANIMENTS

Fresh vegetables play an important role in our high-energy diet. They are rich in vitamins, minerals, and other vital nutrients. Garden-fresh vegetables are the most flavorful and nutritious and are always our first choice. Grow your own if you can, or seek out a market that sells locally grown produce. Choose the vegetables that are in season.

Many a delicious and nutritious vegetable has been rendered virtually worthless by overcooking. Most people who think they don't like vegetables have tasted only the overcooked canned or frozen varieties, which bear little resemblance to their crisp and flavorful fresh beginnings. Most vegetables require very little cooking. Organize your meal preparation time so that everything is ready to serve as soon as the vegetables are done. If your vegetables are already in the steamer on the stove, you can simply turn on the burner a few minutes before the rest of the meal is ready for the table.

We don't limit vegetables to the role of side dishes, but in some meals, vegetables do play a minor part. The recipes in this chapter provide some ideas for those times.

Herb Companions for Vegetables

Some herbs combine well, others are better alone. As a general rule, an herb which imparts a subtle flavor is best used alone or combined with other subtle herbs, as a strong-flavored herb will overpower it. Experiment to see which flavors tantalize your taste buds.

Explore vegetable/herb combinations. The following list is a guide. Use it as a starting point for experimentation.

Asparagus: dill weed, nutmeg
Artichokes: dill weed, curry, mustard
Avocado: chili powder, cilantro
Beets: citrus peel, caraway seeds, mustard, ginger, cloves, dill seed, mint
Beans, green: summer savory, chives, nutmeg, basil
Broccoli: mustard, nutmeg, curry ginger
Brussels sprouts: caraway seed, celery seed, mustard
Cabbage, green or white: caraway seed, celery seed, mustard
Cabbage, red: nutmeg, cloves, mint
Carrots: anise, nutmeg, chives, parsley, curry, mint, ginger, dill weed
Cauliflower: ground mustard, paprika, dill, tarragon, curry, caraway, nutmeg
Corn: cumin, nutmeg, curry spices
Cucumber: dill weed, basil, celery seed
Eggplant: basil, oregano, chives, parsley, paprika, curry spices, caraway seeds, ginger
Leeks: dill weed, curry spices, mustard, tarragon
Mushrooms: thyme, paprika, parsley, chives, oregano
Onions: sorrel, curry spices, cumin
Peas: rosemary, mint, parsley

Potatoes: dill weed, parsley, mustard, mint, rosemary, poppy seed, celery seed, caraway seed, paprika, chives, curry spices, savory

Spinach: curry spices, nutmeg, dill weed

Sweet potatoes or yams: cinnamon, nutmeg, cloves, ginger

Squash (acorn, butternut, and other winter varieties): cinnamon, nutmeg, cloves, ginger, basil, oregano

Squash (crookneck, zucchini, and other summer varieties): oregano, savory, curry spices, ginger, basil

Standard seasonings for green salads: tarragon, dill, basil, parsley

Tomatoes: basil, chives, oregano, nutmeg, tarragon, thyme

VEGETABLE STEAMING TIMES

Artichokes, whole	35 minutes
Beans, green	9 minutes
Beets, medium whole	20–25 minutes
Broccoli	10 minutes
Brussels sprouts, whole	15 minutes
Cabbage, wedges	9 minutes
Carrots, medium slices	10 minutes
Cauliflower, whole	15 minutes
Cauliflower, flowerets	10 minutes
Corn, fresh kernels or ears	8 minutes
Onions, boiling	20 minutes
Peas, edible pod or shelled	8 minutes
Potatoes, small chunks	12 minutes
Rutabagas, small chunks	18 minutes
Spinach and other greens	3–4 minutes
Summer squash	8 minutes
Yams or sweet potatoes, 1-inch thick pieces	30 minutes

SPECIFIC POINTERS

▶ Most vegetables needn't be peeled, and there is truth to the rumor that valuable nutrients are thrown away with the skins. Simply scrub root vegetables well to remove all traces of soil. Other vegetables can be rinsed or gently wiped before cooking. In the rare cases where peeling is desirable, the recipe will say so.

▶ You're certain to discover some favorite vegetable medleys—combinations of textures, flavors, and colors that especially please you. When sautéing or steaming a medley, start the vegetables that require the longest cooking first and add the quicker-cooking ones as the clock counts down. As a general guideline, dense root vegetables require the most cooking, the more delicate flowers and seedpods require a moderate (but variable) cooking time, and leafy vegetables take only moments.

▶ Steaming is the preferred way to cook any vegetable. All you need is a steaming tray and a pot with a tight-fitting lid that's large enough to accommodate the tray. The vegetable pieces are placed on the tray inside the pot and are steamed over medium heat until slightly tender but not soft. We've provided a table here for steaming times, but remember, these times are approximate: cooking time depends to some degree on the size of the pieces you're steaming. We recommend removing the lid toward the end and gently piercing the vegetable with a fork to find out just when it is done to perfection.

Tarragon Steamed Artichokes with Dill Dip

Preparation time: 30 minutes
Prepare one artichoke per person

    Artichokes
    Water
1 tsp vinegar
1 small bay leaf
1 tsp tarragon
    Dash cayenne pepper
⅓ cup mayonnaise
⅓ cup sour cream
1 tsp dill weed

Trim off all but about 1 inch of the stem. Peel off a couple of rows of bottom leaves. Slice through the pointy end of artichokes to remove about ½ inch. Halve the artichokes lengthwise. Meanwhile heat an inch of water to boiling in a tightly covered kettle. Add the vinegar, bay leaf, tarragon, and cayenne. Insert steaming tray and lay artichoke halves on it, cut side down. Cover tightly and steam over medium heat for about 25 minutes, or until fork-tender (but not limp) at base. Mix the mayonnaise, sour cream, and dill weed. Serve hot artichokes with the dipping sauce, providing a separate plate or bowl for discarded leaves.

Cooked Beets

Special requirement: a pressure cooker
Preparation time: 25 minutes
Makes: 4 servings

2 lbs fresh beets with greens
    Quick Rarebit Sauce (page 92)
    optional,
    or Tahini Miso Sauce (page 90) optional

Twist the greens from the beets and set aside. Heat an inch of water in a pressure cooker. When it boils, insert a vegetable steamer and place beets in it. Cover and bring to steaming. Pressure cook for 10—12 minutes, depending on size of beets. Remove from heat and let cool before removing lid. Meanwhile, wash and tear beet greens, discarding stems. Remove beets from pressure cooker and put the greens in. Cover and return to high heat only until steam comes up. Remove from heat. Slide beets out of their skins and slice them. Mound steamed greens on either end of a platter or other serving dish; arrange beet slices in the center. Drizzle Quick Rarebit Sauce or Tahini Miso Sauce over beets and greens, or serve plain with lemon wedges. You may cook the beets without a pressure cooker by steaming in a kettle with a tight-fitting lid for about 35—40 minutes or unti beets are fork-tender.

Brussels Sprouts with Sour Cream

Preparation time: 20 minutes
Makes: 4 servings

   1 lb brussels sprouts
   ½ cup sour cream
   2 Tbsp butter, melted
   2 Tbsp lemon juice

Wash the brussels sprouts and trim the ends, removing any tough outer leaves. Place in a saucepan on a steaming tray over an inch of water. Steam until al dente, about 15 minutes. Meanwhile, combine the sour cream, butter, and lemon juice. Transfer the brussels sprouts to a warm serving dish and toss with the sour cream mixture. Serve very hot.

Mashed Potatoes

Preparation time: 20 minutes
Makes: 2 servings

2–3 potatoes, peeled and cubed
   3 Tbsp butter
   ½ cup milk
   3 Tbsp Parmesan cheese
   1 chopped green onion

Boil the potatoes until tender; drain well. Mash them and blend in the butter, milk, and cheese. Add the green onion, stir, and serve.

Sunshine Cauliflower

Preparation time: 30 minutes
Makes: 4 servings

   1 medium cauliflower
   ⅓ cup mayonnaise
   2 tsp Dijon mustard
      or regular prepared mustard
   ¾ cup grated cheddar cheese
      Parsley for garnish (optional)

Wash the cauliflower; remove the leaves and trim the base. Steam over an inch of water for 15 minutes or until just tender. While the cauliflower is cooking, mix together the mayonnaise and mustard in a small bowl. Preheat oven to 375°. When the cauliflower is fork-tender, place in a shallow casserole dish. Pour the mayonnaise/mustard mixture over the top, and sprinkle on the cheese. Bake, uncovered, for about 10 minutes or until the cheese melts. Serve immediately, garnished with sprigs of fresh parsley.

Carrots with Tarragon

Preparation time: 15 minutes
Makes: 4 to 6 servings

- 4 large carrots
- 3 Tbsp butter
- 1 tsp dried tarragon, crumbled
- 1 clove garlic, minced
  Dash salt
  Dash pepper

Peel the carrots and slice them slantwise. Steam the carrots over an inch of water until al dente, about 10 minutes. Melt the butter in a large frying pan and add the tarragon, garlic, salt, and pepper. Add the carrots and stir for several seconds. Serve immediately.

Gingered Carrots and Broccoli

Preparation time: 15 minutes
Makes: 4 to 6 servings

- 2 Tbsp butter
- 1 tsp powdered ginger
- 1 bunch broccoli (about 3 cups), chopped
- 2 medium carrots, sliced
- 1 tsp honey
- ¼ cup white wine
- 1 tsp arrowroot powder
- 2 Tbsp water

Melt the butter in a large skillet over low heat. Stir in the ginger, broccoli, and carrots. Pour in the wine. Cover and simmer over low heat for 5 minutes. Mix the arrowroot with the water and stir in. Continue cooking 3 to 4 more minutes, or until fork-tender. Serve immediately. These vegetables are good served with curry dishes, or at a holiday feast.

Lemony Apples and Carrots

Preparation time: 15 minutes
Makes: 4 servings

- 2 cups carrots
- 1 large Pippin apple
- 1 Tbsp sesame oil
- 2 tsp grated lemon peel
- 1 tsp lemon juice
- 1 tsp tamari soy sauce
- ½ cup grated mild cheddar cheese (optional)

Scrub the carrots and, without peeling, thinly slice them. Wash and core the apple and, without peeling, cut it into ½-inch cubes. Steam apples and carrots for 5 minutes. Meanwhile combine the oil, lemon peel and juice, and tamari in a skillet and simmer over low heat. When apples and carrots are tender-crisp, drain them and add them to the skillet. Stir over low heat for a few minutes. Serve as is or sprinkle with grated cheese and run under broiler until cheese melts.

Steamed Carrots

Preparation time: 15 minutes
Makes: 4 servings

- 4 medium carrots
- 2 Tbsp butter
- ¼ cup sour cream
  Dash ground ginger or chili powder

Peel the carrots and slice them slantwise. Steam until al dente, about 10 minutes. Transfer immediately to a warm serving bowl and toss with the remaining ingredients. Serve at once. Yogurt may be substituted for the sour cream—it's particularly good with the ginger seasoning.

Green Beans with Sunflower Seeds

Preparation time: 15 minutes
Makes: 4 servings

- 1 lb green beans, sliced
- 2 Tbsp butter
- ½ cup sunflower seeds
- 1 tsp tamari soy sauce
- ½ cup sour cream

Wash the beans and cut them slantwise into ½-inch pieces. Steam until al dente, about 10 minutes. Meanwhile, melt the butter in a small pan. Sauté the sunflower seeds for about 5 minutes, stirring frequently. Add the tamari and sour cream, and heat through over low heat. When the beans are cooked, add them to tamari—sour cream mixture and stir well to coat. Transfer to a warm serving bowl and serve immediately. This dish also makes an excellent cold salad.

Au Gratin Potatoes

Preparation time: 30 minutes to assemble, then 40 minutes to bake
Makes: 4 to 6 servings

- 4 large potatoes, sliced
- 1 small onion, sliced
- 1½ cups cheddar cheese, grated
- 1 cup milk
- 4 Tbsp butter
- 2 tsp whole wheat flour
- ¼ tsp bakon yeast
- ½ tsp salt
- ⅛ tsp pepper
  Parsley (for garnish)

Preheat oven to 350°. Slice the potatoes about ¼-inch thick. Butter a glass 3-quart baking dish and layer the potatoes, alternating with the onion and cheese. End with a layer of potatoes. In a saucepan melt the butter. Stir in the flour, bakon yeast, salt, and pepper. Slowly stir in the milk and cook at a simmer until mixture begins to thicken. Pour over the potatoes. Bake, covered, for 30 minutes, then uncover and bake 10 more minutes. Serve topped with freshly chopped parsley.

Brussels Sprouts with Nutmeg

Preparation time: 20 minutes
Makes: 2—3 servings

     12 brussels sprouts
      2 Tbsp butter
         Dash nutmeg

Wash the brussels sprouts and trim the ends, removing any tough outer leaves. Place in a saucepan on a steaming tray over an inch of water. Cover tightly; bring to a boil and reduce heat to a simmer. Steam for about 15 minutes, until they are al dente. Remove from heat and transfer to a warm serving dish. Toss with the butter and ground or grated nutmeg. Serve immediately.

Parmesan Potatoes

Preparation time: 35 minutes
Makes: 6 to 8 servings

      4 large russet potatoes
      ½ cup yogurt
      ½ cup freshly grated Parmesan cheese
      2 tsp prepared spicy mustard
      1 tsp sea salt
         Paprika

Scrub the potatoes. Without peeling, cut them into small cubes, and steam for 15—20 minutes or until very tender. In a large bowl or pot, whip the potatoes with the yogurt, cheese, mustard, and salt until perfectly smooth. Pour into a 1-quart baking dish, sprinkle generously with paprika, and broil until the top is slightly brown. Serve immediately, perhaps with a spicy vegetable stew or with grilled fish.

Scalloped Potatoes

Preparation time: 15 minutes to assemble,
     then 65 minutes to bake
Makes: 4 to 6 servings

    6 medium potatoes
    4 Tbsp butter
    4 Tbsp flour
      Salt and pepper
    2 cups milk

Preheat oven to 350°. Butter the bottom and sides of a 3-quart casserole dish. Scrub the potatoes and slice into ¼-inch slices. Assemble in 4 layers in the casserole dish: dot each layer with ¼ of the butter and sprinkle evenly with ¼ of the flour. To each layer add salt and pepper to taste. After the last layer, pour the milk over the potatoes. Bake, covered, about 55 minutes or until bubbly, then uncover and bake an additional 10 minutes or until top is slightly brown.

Whipped Yams

Preparation time: about 30 minutes
Makes: 4 servings

    2 large yams (about ¾ lb)
    3 Tbsp buttermilk
    2 tsp tamari soy sauce
    ½ tsp honey
    ¼ tsp nutmeg
    ¼ tsp ground ginger
    1 Tbsp butter or vegetable oil
      Mint leaves for garnish (optional)

Scrub the yams well and, without peeling, dice. Pressure cook for 8 minutes or steam for 20 minutes. Meanwhile, whisk together the buttermilk, tamari, honey, and spices. Set aside. When yams are very tender, drain, and remove to mixing bowl. Add the butter or vegetable oil and mash with a masher or a fork. Now add buttermilk mixture and whip with a fork. Yams should be fluffy and homogeneous. Serve hot, perhaps heaped in a bowl and garnished with fresh mint leaves.

Debbie's Creamy Zucchini Curry

Preparation time: 15 minutes
Makes: 4 servings

  2 Tbsp butter
  ½ onion, thinly sliced
  2 cloves garlic, minced
  2 medium zucchini, sliced
  1 tsp curry powder
  1 pint sour cream
     Salt and black pepper to taste

Heat the butter over low heat in a skillet. Sauté the onion and garlic in the butter until onion becomes limp (about 5 minutes). Slice the zucchini ⅛-inch thick and add to the skillet. Sprinkle in the curry powder. Sauté until zucchini becomes somewhat limp, about 7 minutes. Add the sour cream and salt and pepper to taste. Stir over very low heat until just heated through, and serve.

Spicy Summer Squash

Preparation time: 10 minutes
Makes: 2 to 4 servings

3–4 cups summer squash, thinly sliced
  ½ medium onion, thinly sliced
  1 Tbsp butter
  ⅓ cup sour cream
  1 tsp chili powder
     Dash of salt

Steam the squash and onion together until just tender, about 7 minutes. Transfer to a warm bowl and stir in the butter, sour cream, chili powder, and salt. Serve immediately.

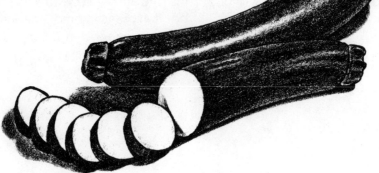

8 GRAIN AND PASTA ACCOMPANIMENTS

For many Americans, potatoes are the preferred carbohydrate course at mealtime. Potatoes are indeed tasty and satisfying, but you miss some delightful flavor combinations if you ignore the infinite possibilities offered by grains and pastas. In Chapter 9, "Main Courses", we offer some of our favorite grain and pasta dishes, suitable for a starring role in a meal. Here we offer those dishes that do wonderfully as a hearty accompaniment to round out an otherwise light meal. Fish entrées and special vegetable dishes are often complemented by a simple and delicious grain or pasta.

SPECIFIC POINTERS

▶ Add a tablespoonful of oil to the cooking water before adding pasta. This prevents noodles from sticking to each other or to the pot.

▶ When pasta is al dente, drain immediately and rinse with cool water to stop cooking. Pasta can be put in a colander in a kettle of warm water if it's not to be served immediately.

▶ Store dry pasta in an airtight container out of direct sunlight. It will stay fresh for several weeks. Freshly made pasta may be frozen, then thawed before cooking.

Rice with Parsley

Preparation time: 40 minutes
Makes: 4 servings

    3 Tbsp butter
    ¼ cup chopped onion or
       4 green onions, chopped
    1 cup long-grain brown rice
    1½ cups water
    ½ tsp salt
    ¼ cup chopped fresh parsley

Sauté the onion in butter in a medium-sized saucepan. Add rice and stir for a few seconds. Add water and salt and bring to a boil. Cover, reduce heat, and simmer until the rice is tender and the water has been absorbed, 30—35 minutes. Stir in parsley, and serve.

Variation: Stir in ½ cup of Parmesan cheese just before serving.

Saffron Rice

Preparation time: 45 minutes
Makes: 4 to 6 servings

    2 Tbsp butter
    1 tsp saffron
    ½ tsp cinnamon
    1 tsp honey
    1 cup long-grain brown rice
    2½ cups water

Melt butter in a saucepan and stir in the saffron, cinnamon, and honey. Stir for several seconds, then add rice. Stir to coat. Pour in water and bring to a boil. Cover; reduce heat and simmer for 35 minutes. This is a good rice dish with a curry dinner.

Spanish Rice

Preparation time: 45 minutes
Makes: 4 servings

    1 Tbsp butter
    ½ medium onion, chopped
    1 tsp chili powder
    ½ tsp cumin
    1 cup brown rice
    1 (canned) chopped green chile pepper
    2 cups water
    ½ tsp salt
    ½ tsp vegetable broth powder
    2 Tbsp tomato purée

Heat the butter in a saucepan with a tight-fitting lid. Sauté the onion in the butter with chili powder and cumin for a couple of minutes, stirring. Add the rice and green chile and continue stirring and sautéing for another couple of minutes. Add the water, salt, vegetable broth powder, and tomato purée and stir. Cover and simmer over low heat for 35 minutes. Stir again and serve.

Fried Rice

Preparation time: 45 minutes
Makes: 4 to 6 servings

    2½ cups water
    1 cup long-grain brown rice
    1 Tbsp oil
    ½ cup finely chopped vegetables (bell pepper, celery, water chestnuts, etc.)
    ½ tsp honey
    1 tsp wine
    1 Tbsp tamari soy sauce
    1 egg, beaten
    1 cup sliced lettuce
    2 Tbsp chopped green onion

Bring the water to a boil and stir in the rice. Return to a boil, then cover and simmer until rice is tender and water is absorbed, about 30—35 minutes. After rice is cooked, heat oil over medium-high heat in a wok or cast-iron frying pan. Sauté the vegetables a few minutes, then stir in the rice. Add honey, wine and tamari. Mix well, using a spatula. Move the mixture to the sides of the pan and scramble the egg in the middle, then stir into the rice mixture. Add the lettuce and stir-fry for 1 minute. Serve immediately, garnished with chopped green onion.

Curried Rice Pilaf

Preparation time: 45 minutes
Makes: 4 servings

- 1 Tbsp butter
- ½ onion, finely chopped
- 2 tsp curry powder
- 1½ cups brown rice
- 3 cups water
- ½ tsp salt
- 1 tsp vegetable broth powder
- ¼ cup sliced green onions or minced parsley (optional)
- 2 Tbsp sunflower seeds or slivered almonds (optional)

Melt the butter in a medium-sized saucepan. Add the onion and curry powder and sauté over low heat until onion becomes limp. Add the raw rice and stir for a minute or two while it sautés. Add the water, salt, and vegetable broth powder. Increase heat until water comes just to boiling. Reduce to low heat; cover tightly and simmer for 35 minutes. Turn off heat and let stand for a few minutes. Toss with the onions or parsley, and nuts, if desired.

Curry-Rice Casserole

Preparation time: 35 minutes for rice, 10 minutes, then 25 minutes to bake
Makes: 4 to 6 servings

- 1 Tbsp butter
- 2½ cups water
- 1 cup long-grain brown rice
- 1 package (10 oz) frozen peas, thawed
- 1 cup sour cream
- 1 cup diced celery
- ¼ cup minced onion
- 2 tsp curry powder
- ½ tsp salt
- ½ tsp dry mustard

Heat water to boiling. Add butter and rice and bring back to boiling; cover tightly and reduce heat to a slow simmer. Cook for 35 minutes or until all water is absorbed. Meanwhile, preheat oven to 350° and butter a 1-quart baking dish. Combine the cooked rice with all remaining ingredients in a large bowl. Blend thoroughly. Spoon into the baking dish and bake, uncovered, for 25 minutes. Delicious hot, this dish can also be served cold.

Bulghur-Millet Pilaf

Preparation time: 30 minutes
Makes: 4 to 6 servings

- 3 cups water
- 1 cup bulghur
- ½ cup millet
- ½ tsp salt
- 1 tsp powdered saffron
- ¼ cup raisins or currants (optional)

Bring the water to a boil in a covered saucepan. Stir in all ingredients, cover tightly, and simmer over low heat for 20 minutes. For the fluffiest pilaf, leave grains in the covered pot for a few minutes after cooking is complete. Then stir with a fork and serve piled on a platter. Surround the pilaf with steamed vegetables and pass your favorite sauce, or smother the mild-flavored pilaf with a spicy vegetable sauté.

Poppy Seed Noodles

Preparation time: 15 to 20 minutes
Makes: 4 servings as a side dish

- ½ lb egg noodles
- 4 Tbsp butter
- 2 Tbsp poppy seeds

Cook noodles in boiling water until al dente. Drain and transfer to a large warm bowl. Toss with the butter, then sprinkle with the poppy seeds.

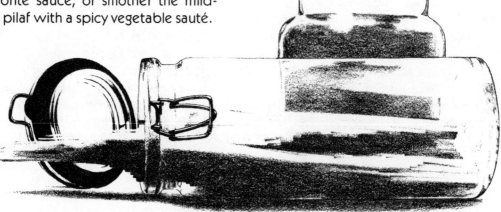

Polenta with Cheese

Preparation time: 20 minutes
Makes: 4 servings

    1¼ cups finely ground yellow cornmeal
     1 cup cold water
     1 tsp salt
    3½ cups water for boiling
     1 cup packed, grated cheddar cheese

Combine the cornmeal, cold water, and salt in a bowl and stir to a uniform paste consistency. Bring 3½ cups water to a boil in a saucepan. As soon as it boils, pour in the cornmeal mixture, lower heat to very low, and beat constantly with a wire whisk while it cooks and thickens, 10—12 minutes. When it reaches the consistency of a thick oatmeal, remove from heat and stir in the grated cheese. When the mixture is smooth, serve very hot. This is a wonderful accompaniment to a spicy vegetable dish.

Chive-Parmesan Noodles

Preparation time: 20 minutes
Makes: 4 servings as a side dish

    ½ lb noodles
    4 Tbsp butter
    ½ cup Parmesan cheese
      Chopped chives

Cook the noodles in boiling water until al dente. Drain and transfer to a large warm bowl. Toss with the butter and cheese, then sprinkle with chives.

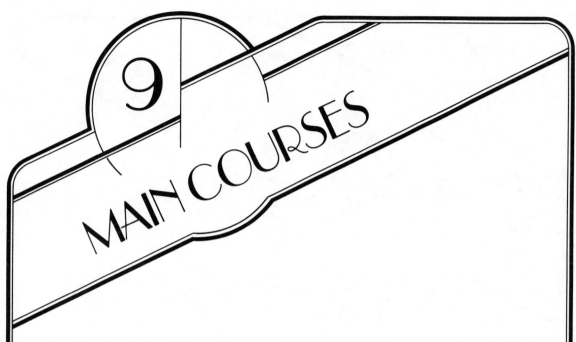

9

MAIN COURSES

What makes a dish a main course? Usually it is a show-stopper, requiring more ingredients and somewhat more elaborate preparation than the dishes that accompany it. Any particularly wonderful dish can be the starring attraction at a meal.

Our main course recipes in this book divide themselves into four categories: vegetables, pasta, tofu, and fish or seafood. We provide a separate introduction to each category, including information about specific ingredients and cooking techniques.

The main courses we've selected are hearty and delicious, and bound to delight even a stalwart meat eater.

VEGETABLE MAIN COURSES

A vegetable entrée is a good choice when you want to serve a light meal. Usually a cooked grain or fresh baked muffins, and a refreshing green salad are perfect accompaniments. When building a meal around a vegetable, freshness is absolutely essential. Allow whatever's in season to inspire your menu plan.

Some vegetable main dishes are sparked by international themes; others are born by creatively combining vegetables and seasonings in a special sauce. In this relatively uncharted territory, experimentation is the rule. We hope our selections inspire you to explore the possibilities on your own.

For specific pointers about vegetables, see Chapter 7.

Greens and Grains

Preparation time: 40 minutes
Makes: 4 servings

  2 cups water
  1 cup dry bulghur wheat
    or millet (or half of each)
    Salt
  2 Tbsp butter
  1 onion, chopped
  2 cloves garlic, minced
  3 cups packed, washed, and torn greens
    (chard, mustard, spinach, or a
    combination)
  1 Tbsp tamari soy sauce
  1 tsp ground nutmeg
  2 tsp basil
  1 Tbsp olive oil
  ½ cup grated Parmesan
  ½ cup grated cheddar cheese

Bring the water to a boil in a medium-sized saucepan. Add the dry grains and a pinch of salt and return to a boil. Cover and simmer over very low heat for 20 minutes. Meanwhile, melt the butter over low heat in a large, deep skillet. Sauté the onion and garlic in the butter for about 10 minutes while you wash and tear the greens, discarding the stems. Do not dry the greens, as the water that clings to them will be what steams them. Add the tamari, nutmeg, and basil to the skillet, then pile in the greens. Cover tightly and cook over low heat for 10 minutes, then uncover and stir to combine cooked greens with the seasonings. Remove from the heat and keep covered. When the grains have cooked for 20 minutes, remove from heat and let sit for 5 minutes without removing the lid. Now toss the cooked grains with the olive oil, then with the greens and cheeses in a serving dish until the cheese melts and everything is well combined. Serve immediately.

Mushroom Stroganoff

Preparation time: 30 minutes
Makes: 4 servings

- 6 Tbsp butter
- 4 cups sliced mushrooms (16—20 fresh mushrooms)
- ½ cup chopped onion
- 2 cloves garlic, minced
- 2 Tbsp whole wheat pastry flour
- 1 Tbsp tomato paste or catsup
- 1 cup stock, heated
- ½ cup sour cream
- 2 Tbsp white wine
- 8 oz egg noodles

Melt 4 tablespoons of the butter in a medium-sized skillet and sauté the mushrooms, onion, and garlic until the onion is golden and the mushrooms are limp, about 20 minutes. Meanwhile, put a large covered saucepan with 3 quarts of salted water on to boil for the noodles. Pour in the dried noodles when the water is rapidly boiling, stir, and let them cook for 8—10 minutes while you complete the sauce.

In a separate large skillet, melt 2 tablespoons of butter over medium-low heat. Stir in the flour and cook for 3 minutes, stirring frequently, then add the tomato paste and the hot stock. Stir well until smooth and thickened. Add the sour cream and stir until well blended. Fold in the mushroom mixture, and add the wine. Combine well and allow to heat through while you drain the cooked noodles. Toss the noodles with a little butter in a warmed, shallow serving dish or on a large warmed platter. Spoon the stroganoff sauce on top.

122

Mushrooms Paprika

Preparation time: 20 minutes
Makes: 4 servings

    1 lb fresh mushrooms
    1 onion
    2 Tbsp butter
    ½ tsp salt
       Dash cayenne pepper
    ½ cup whipping cream
    2 Tbsp sour cream
    1 Tbsp sherry
    1 tsp paprika
       Crisp toast

Clean the mushrooms, leaving stems intact, and cut into thin slices. Cut the onion in half lengthwise, then thinly slice each half. Heat the butter in a skillet. Add the onion; sauté over medium heat for a few minutes, stirring frequently, until onion is golden and becoming limp. Add the mushrooms, salt, and cayenne pepper and sauté until mushrooms are tender, about 8 to 10 minutes. Add the cream, sour cream, sherry, and paprika and stir until heated through. Serve over crisp toast triangles.

Fresh Tomato and Squash Sauté

Preparation time: 25 minutes
Makes: 2 to 4 servings

    3½ cups chopped tomatoes
    4–5 Tbsp olive oil
      1 medium onion, sliced
      2 cloves garlic, minced
      1 tsp basil
      3 cups sliced zucchini
         or other summer squash

If using fresh tomatoes, blanch by placing in boiling water until the skins split; cool under running water, peel, and discard the skins. Chop the tomatoes, saving any juice that runs off. Sauté the onion and garlic until golden in the olive oil in a skillet over low heat. Add the basil, stirring to coat the onion. Add the tomatoes, their juice, and the squash; cook over medium heat until the squash is just tender.

This dish is good over noodles or steamed rice. Adding grated Parmesan cheese at the end makes a pleasant variation.

Chinese Vegetables

Preparation time: 20 minutes
Makes: 6 servings
Serve with: steamed rice

      2 Tbsp oil
      2 cups chopped celery
      2 cups chopped broccoli
      2 cups sliced carrots
      1 cup snow peas
      1 cup chopped onion
      2 cups water
      3 Tbsp arrowroot powder
      3 Tbsp tamari soy sauce
      1 tsp ground ginger

Heat the oil in a wok or deep skillet over high heat. Add the vegetables and stir until hot, about 10 minutes. Combine the water, arrowroot powder, tamari, and ginger, whisking to dissolve the arrowroot or shaking vigorously in a jar with a tight-fitting lid. Pour over the vegetables. Heat and stir until sauce is thickened and vegetables are slightly tender (about 5 minutes). Serve very hot with steamed rice.

Spicy Stir-Fried Vegetables

Preparation time: 25 minutes
Makes: 4 to 6 servings
Serve with: cooked grains or noodles

- 2 Tbsp butter
- 2 cloves garlic, minced
- 6 green onions, sliced into half-inch lengths
- ¼ tsp crushed red chili peppers (or more, if you like very spicy food)
- 3 cups chopped broccoli
- 1–2 carrots, thinly sliced
- 1 cup water
- 1 cup sliced fresh mushrooms

Sauce:

- 1 cup water
- 1 Tbsp tamari soy sauce
- ½ tsp ground ginger
- 2 Tbsp arrowroot powder

Melt the butter in a deep skillet or wok that has a tight-fitting lid. Add the garlic, onions, and chili pepper. Stir briefly, then add the broccoli and carrots and stir to coat vegetables with the butter and seasonings. Pour in one cup of water. Cover and cook over high heat for 5 minutes. Remove lid and reduce heat to a simmer. Add the mushrooms and continue to simmer, stirring occasionally, until broccoli is tender-crisp (5 to 10 minutes). Liquid should be almost gone. Meanwhile, stir together the sauce ingredients. When vegetables are done, pour this mixture into the skillet all at once and stir briefly over low heat until sauce thickens and coats vegetables. Serve hot with cooked grains or noodles.

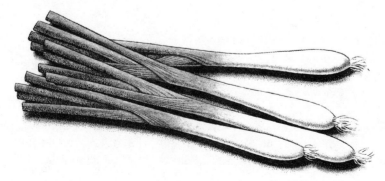

Vegetable Curry

Preparation time: 30 minutes
Makes: 4 to 6 servings

- 1 medium cauliflower
- 2 medium carrots
- 1 large potato
- 3 Tbsp butter
- 1 onion
- 2 cloves garlic, minced
- 2½ tsp curry powder
- 1¼ cups water
- ½ tsp salt
  Cayenne pepper (optional)
- 2 fresh tomatoes, coarsely chopped
- ¼ cup minced fresh parsley
- ¼ cup thinly sliced green onions
- ½ lemon, juiced

Chop the cauliflower into small and medium flowerets. Scrub and cut the carrots into thick slices. Peel and chop the potato. Melt the butter in a large pot that has a tight-fitting lid. Slice, or chop, the onion and sauté with the garlic and curry powder, in the butter, for 2 minutes, stirring. Then add the cauliflower, carrots, and potato. Stir to coat the vegetables with curry, then add the water and salt (and some cayenne, if you enjoy a hot curry). Cover and cook over medium-high heat for 10 minutes.

Remove lid. Add the tomatoes and cook, uncovered, for a few minutes longer, until the tomatoes are heated through and the other vegetables are tender-crisp. Remove from heat; stir in the parsley, green onions, and lemon juice. Serve very hot, perhaps with a grain pilaf and a crunchy vegetable salad. The following suggestions for condiments will complete any curry dinner.

Curry Condiments

Provide small dishes of:

Raisins or dates
Shredded coconut
Plain yogurt
Cashew pieces
Peanuts
Chutney, spicy and sweet
Banana chunks (sprinkled with lemon juice to prevent darkening)

These condiments can be grouped in the center of the table within everyone's reach. Each guest combines flavors as desired. Share and enjoy!

Stuffed Acorn Squash

Preparation time: 30 minutes to assemble,
  then 15 to bake
Makes: 4 servings

    2 acorn squash
    8 tsp butter, softened
    1 can (1 lb) chunk pineapple, drained
    ¼ cup honey
    2 Tbsp dark rum
    ½ tsp ground cinnamon or
       pumpkin pie spice (page 32)
    ½ cup chopped walnuts or pecans

Preheat oven to 350°. Cut each squash in half and remove the seeds. Place halves in a large pan on a steamer rack and steam for about 20 minutes. Remove from pan and place, cut-side up, in a baking dish. With a fork, pierce the inside of the squash, and then spread 2 teaspoonsful of butter in each half. In a bowl, combine the drained pineapple, honey, rum, spices, and nuts. Divide this mixture among the squashes. Bake in the oven for 15 minutes, or until filling is hot and squash is tender. This dish is a great winter treat.

Ratatouille

Preparation time: 35 minutes
Makes: 4 to 6 servings

    3 Tbsp olive oil
    1 large bell pepper, coarsely chopped
    1 large onion, coarsely chopped
    3 cloves garlic, minced
    1 large eggplant, cubed uniformly
    2 medium zucchini, thickly sliced
    ½ tsp thyme
    ½ tsp oregano
    1 tsp sea salt
       Cayenne pepper
    ½ cup dry red wine
    1 large tomato, finely chopped
    1 tsp honey
    ½ lemon

Heat the oil in a large skillet that has a tight-fitting lid. Sauté the bell pepper, onion, and garlic over medium heat, stirring frequently, for 5 minutes. Add the eggplant and zucchini and sauté for 5 minutes longer. Now add the thyme, oregano, salt, a dash of cayenne, and the wine. Stir well. Cover and simmer over low heat for 20 minutes. Remove cover and add the tomato and honey. Heat through. Squeeze in the lemon, and add a little more salt and cayenne if desired. Serve very hot.

127

Stuffed Artichokes

Preparation time: 45 minutes
Makes: 2 servings

     2 large artichokes
     1 Tbsp minced onion
     5 medium mushrooms, sliced
     1 clove garlic, minced
     1 Tbsp olive oil
    ⅓ cup sour cream
    ½ tsp curry powder
     2 Tbsp white wine
    ½ lb tiny shrimp
    ½ lb coarse dry bread crumbs
        Grated Cheese (optional)

Wash the artichokes, and trim the stem so that they will sit flat. Steam until fork-tender, but not soft, about ½ hour. (If you have a pressure cooker, cook them under pressure for 8—10 minutes.) Cool slightly, to make handling easier. Open out the leaves and use a spoon to scoop out the center thistle fibers, exposing the heart portion underneath. Be careful to remove all the thistles—they're what put the "choke" in "artichoke." While the artichokes are cooking, sauté the onion, mushrooms, and garlic in olive oil until tender. Stir in the sour cream, curry powder, and wine, then add the shrimp. Stir and heat through.

Stir in the bread crumbs and cook until thick. Spoon this mixture into the artichoke cavities. You may wish to top with a little grated cheese or a spoonful of sour cream. Place in individual baking dishes or a small casserole, and bake for 5 minutes at 350°.

Sesame Eggplant

Preparation time: 20 minutes
Makes: 2 servings

    1 medium eggplant
      Dry bread crumbs
    3 Tbsp sesame seeds, toasted*
      Whole wheat pastry flour
    1 egg, beaten
      Sesame oil
      Grated cheese (optional)
      Salsa (optional)

Peel and slice the eggplant into ¼-inch thick slices. Combine the toasted sesame seeds with the bread crumbs on a small plate to a depth of ½ inch. Place about ¼ inch of flour on a separate plate. Dip slices of eggplant first in the flour, then in beaten egg, then in the bread crumb/sesame mixture. Let sit for about 5 minutes while you heat a thin layer of sesame oil in a skillet. Brown the eggplant slices on both sides, top with grated cheese and a spoonful of hot salsa if desired, and put under the broiler just long enough to melt the cheese.

* To toast raw sesame seeds, place in a hot skillet and shake over medium heat until they begin to darken (it takes less than a minute).

Eggplant Patties

Preparation time: 20 minutes
Makes: 4 to 6 servings

    1 medium eggplant
    1¼ cups dry bread crumbs
    1¼ cups grated cheese
    2 eggs, beaten
    2 Tbsp chopped parsley
    2 Tbsp chopped green onion
    1 clove garlic, minced
    ½ tsp salt
    ⅛ tsp black or cayenne pepper
      Oil for frying
      Creamy Herb Sauce (page 90), optional

Peel and cube the eggplant and steam until very tender, about 10 minutes. Drain, then mash with a fork in a large bowl. Add all remaining ingredients, except the oil and Creamy Dill Sauce, and stir until well combined. Flour your palms, and form mixture into patties. Fry in a thin layer of hot oil until golden brown, a few minutes on each side. Serve hot, either plain or with Creamy Dill Sauce.

Mushroom Tacos or Tostadas

Preparation time: 30 minutes
Makes: 8 tacos or tostadas

      2 Tbsp butter
      2 large cloves garlic
      1 medium onion
      ¾ lb fresh mushrooms
      2 tsp chili powder
      1 tsp oregano
      ½ tsp salt
      1 tsp tamari soy sauce
      2 tsp fresh lemon juice
      ½ tsp Bakon yeast
         Dash cayenne pepper
         Oil for frying
   6–8 corn tortillas
      1 ripe avocado, sliced
      ½ pint sour cream
         Shredded lettuce (optional)
         Diced tomato (optional)
         Spanish Rice (page 114)(optional)

Melt the butter in a large skillet over medium heat. Mince the garlic and finely dice the onion; sauté them in the butter over low heat while you wipe the mushrooms clean, trim off the tough stems, and thinly slice the caps. Stir the mushrooms, chili powder, oregano, and salt into the skillet. Cover and cook over low heat for 10 minutes. Remove cover, stir in the tamari, lemon juice, Bakon yeast, and cayenne. Keep hot over very low heat. Heat the oven to 250°. In a small amount of hot oil in a separate skillet, fry the tortillas over medium heat until slightly stiff for tacos, crisp for tostadas. For tacos, fold cooked tortillas in half when you remove them from the frying pan. Distribute filling evenly among tortillas, filling the crease in taco shells or spreading on top of tostada shells. Keep filled shells warm in the oven until ready to serve (no longer than a few minutes). Put the avocado slices on top of the filling and garnish with a dollop of sour cream. If you wish, top tostadas with shredded lettuce and chopped tomato. Serve at once, perhaps with Spanish Rice and a crisp green salad.

Enchiladas

Preparation time: 30 minutes
Makes: 4 to 6 servings

Sesame oil for frying
1 avocado
6 mushrooms
¼ lb cheddar cheese
1 can (8 oz) whole chiles
6 corn tortillas
1 cup Fresh salsa (page 94) or
canned variety
Sour cream

Thinly slice the avocado, mushrooms, cheese, and chiles. Heat a shallow layer of oil in a frying pan over low heat, lightly fry each tortilla in the hot oil, and place on a plate. Fill with mushrooms, cheese, chiles, and avocado, roll, and secure with a tooth-pick. (Reserve several avocado and cheese slices for a garnish, if you wish.) As you fill the tortillas, place them side-by-side in a lightly buttered baking dish. Pour the salsa over the enchiladas and broil for 5 minutes, then bake for 5 minutes at 350°. Serve topped with sour cream.

Chile Relleño Casserole

Special requirement: a blender
Preparation time: 15 minutes to assemble,
then 30 minutes to bake
Makes: 2 to 4 servings

1 can (4 oz) whole chiles
½ lb grated cheese
5 eggs, lightly beaten
2 Tbsp milk or half-and-half
2 Tbsp minced onion
½ tsp salt
2 cloves garlic, minced
Freshly ground pepper
Sour cream (optional)
Salsa (optional)

Preheat oven to 325°. Generously butter a two-quart casserole, and arrange the whole chiles on the bottom. In the blender, combine the cheese, eggs, milk or half-and-half, onion, salt, garlic, and pepper. Mix at low speed for 2 minutes. Slowly pour this mixture over the chiles in the baking dish and bake for 30 minutes. Let cool for a few minutes before serving. This is great served as is, or top with sour cream and hot salsa.

131

Quesadillas

Preparation time: 10 minutes
Prepare 1 to 2 quesadillas per person

For each quesadilla:

Butter for frying
1 flour tortilla
A few thin slices of cheese (Swiss, Jack, or cheddar)
Selected vegetable slices: mushrooms, black olives, bell pepper, avocado, and onions are good choices, individually or in combination
Sour cream
Salsa

Heat 1 tablespoon of butter in a cast-iron skillet over medium-high heat. Thinly slice cheese and whatever vegetables you have selected. (Go easy on the vegetables or you'll end up with a fat burrito instead of a flat quesadilla.) Put a flour tortilla into the skillet and layer a couple of slices of cheese and the vegetables on half of it. Fold the other half over and continue frying until golden brown and crisp, then turn and fry the other side. Repeat this process for each quesadilla, adding more butter as necessary. Serve hot, topped with sour cream and salsa to taste.

Cheese Fondue

Preparation time: 25 minutes
Makes: 4 servings

- ¾ lb Swiss cheese
- 1¾ tsp whole wheat pastry flour
- 1 clove garlic
- ¾ cup dry white wine
- ¼ tsp salt
- Pinch pepper
- ⅛ tsp nutmeg
- French bread, 1-inch cubes

- Assorted Vegetables (for dipping):
- Carrot sticks
- Cauliflower flowerets
- Broccoli stalks
- Green onions
- Cherry tomatoes

Coarsely grate the cheese and toss with the flour. Rub a saucepan and wooden spoon with the garlic. Pour in the wine and heat slowly until very hot, but not boiling. Add the cheese and stir until melted. Stir in the salt, pepper, and nutmeg. When very smooth and well blended, transfer to a warm fondue pot and serve with assorted vegetables and cubes of French bread for dipping.

Fondue is fun to prepare in the presence of guests. Make it a social event as well as a gastronomical delight by inviting guests to prepare the vegetables and grate the cheese. Enjoy taking turns dipping into the fondue, and always serve your favorite white wine to wash it down.

PASTA MAIN COURSES

Spaghetti has become almost as American as apple pie, but there is a whole world of pasta flavors and shapes you may not have discovered—and the sauces for them are limited only by your imagination. Seek out a good Italian market for the largest variety and the best quality pastas.

There is a basic cooking technique that applies to all kinds of pasta. For one pound of dried pasta, bring 4 quarts of water to a boil and add a tablespoonful of oil, to prevent sticking. Drop the pasta into the vigorously boiling pot and stir to see that it separates. When the water returns to a boil, begin watching the clock and cook for several minutes (the package will tell you the approximate cooking time). When the recommended cooking time is almost up, remove one noodle and taste to see if it is done. Continue taste-testing one noodle every minute or so until pasta is perfectly al dente. The literal translation of this Italian phrase is "to the tooth," and it refers to that stage at which pasta is limp and tender, but not soft. It will still be slightly chewy. When this stage is reached, drain immediately and toss with the sauce ingredients you have prepared. One pound of dry pasta will feed six people, so allow 2 to 3 ounces per person when estimating how much to prepare.

Combine sauces and pastas with care. The subtle quality of a delicate sauce can be overpowered by a strong-flavored whole-grain noodle. We've indicated our preference with each specific recipe. Keeping this rule of thumb in mind, you may substitute another type of pasta with different (but just as good) results.

A good pasta, served with a fresh leafy salad and perhaps a crusty garlic bread, will be savored and remembered. Here is a repertoire of recipes with which you can delight your friends.

For specific pointers about pasta, see Chapter 8.

Soba (Buckwheat Noodles) with Fried Vegetables

Preparation time: 25 minutes
Makes: 2 to 3 servings

- 1½ qts water
- ½ tsp salt
- 1 Tbsp miso
- ⅛ cup sesame oil
- 2–3 cloves garlic, minced
- 1 bunch green onions, sliced into 1-inch pieces
- 2 cups broccoli or asparagus, uniformly sliced, or diced
- 6 oz tofu, frozen, then thawed, squeezed dry, and finely diced
- 1 tsp tamari soy sauce
  Cayenne pepper
- 8 oz uncooked soba (buckwheat noodles)
- 1 Tbsp butter
  Sesame seeds for garnish (optional)

Heat the water to a boil in a large kettle with the salt. Whisk miso with 3 tablespoons water until smooth and set aside. In a large skillet or wok, heat the oil over medium heat, then add the garlic, green onions, and broccoli or asparagus. Sauté for 10 minutes, stirring frequently. Stir in the tofu, tamari, and a couple of shakes of cayenne pepper (or more to taste) and sauté for 5 minutes longer. Now turn heat off and stir in miso mixture. Meanwhile, put the soba in the boiling water and boil for 5 minutes. Drain noodles well and toss them with 1 tablespoon butter in a serving dish. Pour vegetables evenly over soba, sprinkle with sesame seeds if you wish, and serve.

Pasta with Cauliflower-Tomato Sauce

Preparation time: 40 minutes
Makes: 4 to 6 servings

- 1 medium cauliflower
- 1 onion, diced
- 2 cloves garlic, minced
- 2 Tbsp butter
- 2 tsp basil
- 1 tsp crushed rosemary
- 6–8 fresh tomatoes, or
  1 large (28-ounce can) tomatoes
- ½ tsp salt
- ¾ lb pasta (thin spaghetti, fettucine, or egg noodles)
- 2 cups sour cream
  Black pepper
  Freshly grated Parmesan cheese

Heat 3 quarts of water to a boil in a large pot. Trim the leaves off the cauliflower, thinly slice the thick stalk pieces, and break the rest into small flowerets. Sauté the cauliflower, onion, and garlic in melted butter in a large deep skillet with basil and rosemary for 10 minutes, stirring occasionally. Meanwhile, if using fresh tomatoes, immerse them in the boiling water until skins split. Remove from the boiling water and plunge into cold water to cool, then slip off the skins. Chop the tomatoes finely, saving any juice that runs off. Add the salt, tomatoes, and their juice to the skillet; cover and simmer over medium heat for 15 minutes.

Meanwhile, cook the pasta in the boiling water (you can use the tomato blanching water) until al dente. When cauliflower is tender-crisp, stir in the sour cream with a few grinds of black pepper. Stir until just heated through; then toss the sauce with the pasta.

Serve immediately, passing the grated Parmesan cheese.

Fettucine Alfredo with Onions and Mushrooms

Preparation time: 35 minutes
Makes: 4 servings

     2 qts water
     4 Tbsp butter
     1 onion
     ½ lb mushrooms
     3 cloves garlic, minced
     2 cups half-and-half
     ½ tsp ground nutmeg
     ¼ tsp salt
       Few grinds black pepper
  8 ~~12~~ oz egg noodles
     1 egg, lightly beaten
     1 cup firmly packed, finely
       grated Parmesan cheese
       Additional grated Parmesan for garnish

Heat the water to a boil in a large pot. Slice the onion in half lengthwise, and thinly slice each half. Wipe the mushrooms clean and thinly slice them. Melt the butter in a large deep skillet, add the onion, mushrooms, and garlic, and sauté over low heat until onions become limp and golden and mushrooms have released their liquid. Add the half-and-half, nutmeg, salt, and pepper. Continue cooking over low heat. Add the noodles to the boiling water and cook about 5 minutes, until al dente. Drain the noodles and rinse under cold running water. At this point, the sauce should be approaching the boiling point. As soon as it starts to boil, add the cooked noodles and stir. Remove from heat. Make a space in the center of the noodles and pour in the lightly beaten egg. Carefully but quickly lift and toss noodles until egg is smoothly mixed with noodles and sauce. Now add the cheese and continue lifting and tossing until the sauce is smooth and well blended and the noodles are evenly coated. Serve immediately, passing more grated cheese and the pepper grinder.

If the fettucine seems more gooey than creamy, add more half-and-half or milk, a little at a time, until the right consistency is reached. A wonderful and easy treat to prepare for guests.

Fettucine al Burro

Preparation time: 30 minutes
Makes: 4—6 servings

  8 cups water
  1 tsp salt
  1 stick (4 oz) butter, softened
  ¼ cup heavy cream
  2 egg yolks
  ½ cup freshly grated Parmesan cheese
  1 lb fettucine noodles
     Additional grated Parmesan cheese

Bring the water to a boil with the salt in a large kettle. Meanwhile, melt the butter in the oven at 250° in a large ovenproof serving bowl. Beat in the cream with a whisk, then add the egg yolks and blend well. Stir in the Parmesan cheese. (Keep warm in oven while the noodles are cooking.) Add the noodles to the boiling water and stir gently with a wooden spoon. Boil until al dente, 5—8 minutes. Drain the noodles well, then add them to the cream and cheese mixture. Toss well to coat, and serve very hot. Pass additional Parmesan cheese, salt, and pepper. Serve with a fresh tossed salad and an antipasto plate.

Pasta with Marinated Egg Sauce

Ahead of time: hard-boil 4 eggs
Preparation time: 15 minutes, plus
      1 hour for flavors to blend
Makes: 3 to 4 servings

  ½ cup olive oil
  ¼ cup dry red wine
  ¼ cup tomato purée
  4 hard-boiled eggs, finely chopped
  2 green onions, finely chopped
  2 cloves garlic, minced
  2 Tbsp minced fresh parsley
  ¼ tsp salt
     Pinch or two of black pepper
  ½ lb vermicelli or egg noodles

Make the sauce by combining all ingredients, except the noodles, in a large bowl. Cover and let stand at room temperature for at least an hour so the flavors can blend. Cook the noodles in 3 quarts lightly salted, boiling water until al dente, 5—8 minutes. Drain the noodles and toss them with the sauce in a large pre-warmed bowl. Serve at once.

Pasta al Pesto

Special requirement: blender or food
         processor
         Preparation time: 40 minutes
         Makes: about 1 cup (serves 4 to 6)

  2 cups fresh basil leaves, firmly packed*
  ½ cup olive oil
  ¾ cup freshly grated Parmesan cheese
  ¼ cup pine nuts (or ½ cup walnut pieces)
  6 garlic cloves
  1 lb fine spaghetti or fettucine
     Additional garlic, olive oil,
     and Parmesan cheese

De-stem, wash, and dry the basil leaves (a salad spinner works well for this). Purée ¼ cup of olive oil in a blender or food processor with the basil, Parmesan cheese, pine nuts, and garlic cloves. With blender or food processor running, add the remaining olive oil in a slow stream. Purée until you have a thick green homogeneous paste.

Cook the pasta in boiling, salted water until al dente, 6—8 minutes. Drain and toss pasta with a drizzle of olive oil in a deep, pre-warmed bowl. Thin the pesto sauce with a couple of tablespoons of hot water; toss gently with the pasta with 2 oiled wooden forks until sauce is evenly distributed. If you really enjoy garlic, you may add a couple of additional cloves (minced) before tossing. Serve immediately and pass plenty of grated Parmesan cheese at the table.

If you don't have a blender or food processor, beg or borrow one. This recipe may take a bit longer the first time you prepare it—the technique is not difficult, just unusual. Using a salad spinner to remove the excess water from the basil leaves as you wash them is a real time saver. If you grow basil in your garden, consider growing enough to make a large batch of pesto to freeze. The Parmesan cheese does not retain its fresh flavor when frozen, so omit it from the original recipe when preparing a batch to freeze and add it to the pesto sauce just before tossing with the noodles. Before putting containers of pesto in the freezer, add a thin film of olive oil on top, to prevent drying.

* Do not use dried basil in this recipe, it does not work.

Stuffed Manicotti

Preparation time: 30 minutes to assemble,
    then 20 minutes to bake
Makes: 4 to 6 servings

Sauce:

 2 Tbsp olive oil
 ½ onion, chopped
 ½ bell pepper, chopped
 1 clove garlic, minced
 2 bay leaves
 1 Tbsp minced fresh parsley
 1 Tbsp oregano, crushed
 1 Tbsp basil, crushed
 2 slices lemon
 1 Tbsp honey
 1 lb fresh or canned tomatoes
 ½ cup dry red wine

Filling:

 6 oz tofu
 1 egg, beaten
 1 cup ricotta cheese
 ¼ cup chopped parsley
 ½ tsp salt
 ¼ cup chopped onion
 ½ cup grated Parmesan cheese
 1 tsp caraway seeds
 10 manicotti shells

Using the sauce ingredients: heat the olive oil in a large pan and sauté the onion, bell pepper, and garlic until tender. Add the herbs and stir, then add the lemon, honey, tomatoes, and red wine. Simmer, uncovered, for about 20 minutes, stirring occasionally.

Meanwhile thinly slice the tofu and place it on several layers of paper towels to absorb excess moisture. In a medium-sized bowl, mix together the beaten egg and the ricotta cheese. Using a fork, mash the tofu on a plate. Stir into the ricotta/egg mixture. Finally, stir in the parsley, salt, chopped onion, Parmesan cheese, and caraway seeds. Fill the uncooked manicotti shells with this mixture. Place half of the sauce in a long, shallow baking dish. Arrange stuffed manicotti in the dish and pour the remaining sauce over them. Bake covered at 400° for 20 minutes.

Lasagna

Preparation times: Sauce—5 minutes to
    assemble, then 30 minutes to simmer
Lasagna—15 minutes to assemble, then
    30 minutes to bake
Makes: 6 servings

Sauce:

¼ cup olive oil
1 onion, minced
1 bell pepper, chopped
2 cloves garlic, minced
1 Tbsp basil
2 bay leaves
½ cup red or white wine
2 thin slices lemon
2 lbs fresh or canned tomatoes
⅓ cup olives, chopped or sliced

1 lb lasagna noodles

Filling:

1 lb tofu
½ lb ricotta cheese
½ cup grated Parmesan cheese
¼ cup white wine
1 Tbsp basil
½ tsp salt
½ cup sour cream

Additional Parmesan cheese

Make the sauce first by heating the olive oil in a large pan, add the onion, bell pepper, and garlic, and sauté until tender. Add the herbs, wine, lemon, tomatoes, and olives. Simmer, uncovered, for 20—30 minutes, stirring occasionally. Meanwhile cook the lasagna noodles in boiling, salted water until al dente, about 10 minutes.

Thinly slice the tofu and place on several layers of paper towels to absorb excess moisture. Mash the tofu in a bowl and add the cheeses, wine, basil, salt, and sour cream; blend well.

To assemble the lasagna, first coat the bottom of a rectangular baking dish with olive oil. Spoon in one-third of the sauce, add a layer of noodles, a layer of the tofu mixture, then more sauce. End with sauce on top. Sprinkle with additional Parmesan cheese. Bake covered for 20 minutes, then uncovered for 10 more minutes or until hot and bubbly. Serve immediately with garlic bread.

For additional pasta recipes see **pasta** in index.

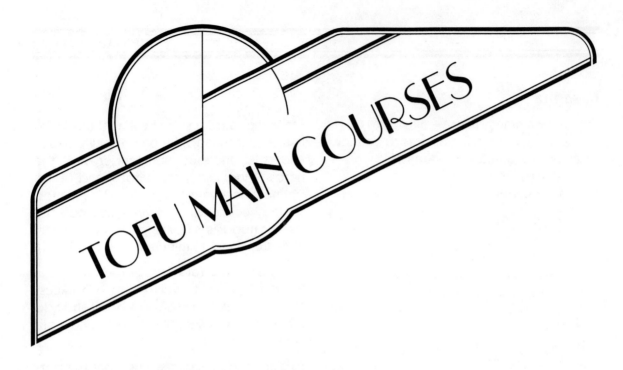

TOFU MAIN COURSES

The increasing interest in tofu as a regular part of the diet is well deserved. It is an excellent source of low-fat, low-calorie, easily digestible protein.

Many people have been exposed to tofu in Oriental cooking, but its bland flavor and subtle texture make it adaptable to many different kinds of seasoning. In addition to the recipes presented here, you'll find tofu as a major ingredient in some of our appetizers, soups, pasta dishes, and even desserts.

Tofu is a cultured soybean derivative, often labeled bean curd. All Asian food stores and most health-food stores carry it, and it is beginning to appear in the produce sections of many major supermarkets.

For many people who choose a meatless diet, tofu has become a staple, and any cook can enjoy using it on occasion, since its versatility is boundless.

SPECIFIC POINTERS

▶ Tofu is usually sold packed in water in a sealed plastic container. Once you've opened the carton, if you change the water daily the tofu will stay fresh for about ten days.

▶ Different tofu manufacturers produce tofu with varying degrees of firmness. Try a couple of brands—you may enjoy the consistency of one more than another.

▶ Unless otherwise stated, soft and firm tofu are pretty much interchangeable in our recipes. You may need to allow soft tofu to drain on paper towels for a few minutes to remove excess water. Where this is necessary, the recipe will advise you.

▶ Frozen and thawed tofu opens a new realm of possibilities. Freezing changes the texture from smooth and custard-like to coarse and spongy. After thawing tofu, gently squeeze out its water, then slice or crumble and use where a chewier, "meaty" texture is desired.

Tofu Sauté

Preparation time: 15 minutes
Makes: 2 servings
Serve with: steamed rice or bulghur

- ½ lb firm tofu
- 2 Tbsp olive oil
- ½ medium red onion, sliced
- 1 bell pepper, chopped
- 2 large mushrooms, sliced
- 1 tsp basil
- 2 Tbsp miso
- ¼ cup fresh chopped parsley
- 1 Tbsp vinegar

Cube the tofu and place on paper towels to remove excess moisture. Heat the oil in a cast-iron skillet and sauté the onion, bell pepper, mushrooms, and basil for 5 minutes. Add the miso and stir until it is dissolved. Then add the parsley, tofu, and vinegar. Sauté for 5 more minutes. Serve very hot. This dish is great accompanied by steamed rice or bulghur.

Tofu Tacos

Preparation time: 25 minutes
Makes: 8 tacos

- 1 Tbsp vegetable oil
- 2 medium onions, coarsely chopped
- 3 cloves garlic, minced
- 1 lb fresh tofu
- 2 Tbsp tamari soy sauce
- 4 Tbsp salsa
- 1 tsp oregano
- 8 Corn tortillas
  Grated cheese (optional)
  Shredded lettuce (optional)
  Chopped tomatoes (optional)

Heat oil in a large skillet over medium heat. Sauté the onion and garlic in the oil, stirring frequently, while you chop the tofu into small cubes. Add the tofu, tamari, salsa, and oregano. Continue stirring and cooking over low heat until most of the liquid is gone. Meanwhile, fry the tortillas in a little vegetable oil until they begin to become crisp. Place a few spoonfuls of filling on each tortilla and top with cheese, lettuce, and tomatoes if you wish. Fold tortilla in half, and serve.

Tofu Burritos

Preparation time: 20 minutes
Makes: 4 to 6 servings

         1-lb tofu, fresh or previously frozen
     ¼ cup chopped onion
     ⅛ cup chopped green pepper
     1 cup tomato sauce
     1 tsp chili powder
     1 tsp cumin
     ½ tsp salt
   2–3 Tbsp oil or butter
  8–10 flour tortillas
    16 slices of cheese
         Fresh salsa (page 94) or
         use a prepared variety of salsa
         Sour cream

If using fresh tofu, rinse and drain off water. Then slice, pat dry with paper towels, and mash in a bowl. If using previously frozen tofu, squeeze out excess water (the tofu will have a sponge-like quality) and crumble it. Combine the tofu with the onion, green pepper, tomato sauce, and spices. Mix well. In a large skillet heat the oil or butter. In the center of each tortilla place a spoonful of the tofu mixture. Top with a couple of slices of cheese, roll, and secure with a toothpick. Place in the frying pan, folded side down. Turn when brown and pour salsa over top. Cover the frying pan and continue to cook 1 minute longer. Serve hot, topped with sour cream.

Sesame Tofu

Preparation time: 15 minutes
Makes: 2 servings
Serve with: steamed rice

    14 oz tofu
     1 egg
     3 Tbsp whole wheat pastry flour
     3 Tbsp sesame seeds
     ½ tsp ground ginger
     2 Tbsp oil
     1 Tbsp tamari soy sauce

Cut the tofu into 1-inch cubes and set aside to blot dry with paper towels. Beat the egg in a bowl. Combine the flour, sesame seeds, and ginger in a shallow dish. Heat the oil in a cast-iron frying pan. Dip the tofu in the egg, then coat evenly with the flour mixture. Fry in the oil over medium heat until evenly browned, turning once or twice. Turn off the heat and pour in the tamari. Toss gently to coat evenly. Serve immediately with steamed rice.

Teriyaki Tofu

Preparation time: 25 minutes
Makes: 4 servings

- 1 lb tofu
- ½ cup flour
- ¼ cup sesame seeds
  Oil for frying
  Chopped green onion

Marinade:

- ⅓ cup tamari soy sauce
- 2 Tbsp dry sherry
- 1 Tbsp molasses
- ¼ tsp ground ginger
- 2 cloves garlic, minced

Rinse and drain the tofu, cut into 1-inch cubes, and pat dry on paper towels. Mix the marinade ingredients together in a shallow bowl. Add the tofu and marinate for 5—10 minutes, turning to coat well. Meanwhile, combine the flour with the sesame seeds. Lift the tofu from the marinade, drain briefly, then dip into the flour mixture to coat all sides. Heat 1 tablespoon of oil in a skillet over medium heat. Add the tofu pieces and brown, turning to cook evenly. Add more oil as needed. Serve immediately, topped with chopped green onion. Use remaining teriyaki sauce for dipping.

Curried Tofu and Onions

Preparation time: 30 minutes
Makes: 4 servings
Serve with: cooked grains or noodles

- 2 Tbsp butter
- 1 onion
- 1 large clove garlic, minced
- 2 tsp curry powder
- 2 cups water
- 1 Tbsp instant vegetable broth powder
- 1 tsp tamari soy sauce
- 10 oz firm tofu
- ½ cup shelled peas (frozen will do)
- 3 Tbsp flour
  Cooked noodles or grain for 4

Heat the butter in a skillet over low heat. Halve the onion lengthwise, and thinly slice each half. Simmer the onions, garlic, and curry powder in the melted butter, stirring occasionally, for 10 minutes. Meanwhile, heat water to a simmer in a covered saucepan, add vegetable broth powder and soy sauce, and keep hot. Slice the tofu into chunks. Add flour to simmering onions and stir for a minute or two, then whisk in hot broth a little at a time. Add tofu and peas and let it bubble, whisking frequently, for 10 minutes or until thickened. Serve over cooked noodles or grain.

Tofu Patties

Preparation time: 40 minutes
Makes: 4 servings

1	cup water
	Pinch of salt
½	cup uncooked bulghur wheat
6	oz tofu (approximately)
2	eggs
2	tsp toasted sesame seeds*
½	medium onion, finely chopped
1	clove garlic, minced
1	tsp Bakon yeast
1	tsp dill weed
1	Tbsp tamari soy sauce
2	Tbsp grated Parmesan cheese
2	Tbsp minced fresh parsley
	Cayenne pepper
½–¾	cup whole wheat pastry flour
	Butter for frying

Bring the water and salt to a boil in a covered medium-sized saucepan. Add the bulghur, lower heat, and simmer with lid ajar until water is absorbed (about 10 minutes). Meanwhile mash the tofu with the eggs (use a whisk if you have one). Add the onion and garlic to tofu along with remaining ingredients except the flour, bulghur, and butter. Mix thoroughly. Add cooked bulghur, and mix again. Now add ½ cup flour and mix again. If mixture is thin, add more flour a little at a time until consistency is thick and sticky. Flour the palms of your hands, and form patties, using 2 tablespoons of the mixture at a time. Fry in a thin layer of butter over low heat for 4—5 minutes per side. Serve plain or with a simple sauce.

* To toast raw sesame seeds, place in a hot skillet and shake over medium heat until they begin to darken. (It takes less than a minute.)

Sweet and Sour Vegetables and Tofu

Preparation time: 30 minutes
Makes: 4 to 6 servings

2 Tbsp butter
½ onion, coarsely chopped
2 cloves garlic, minced
1 large carrot, thinly sliced
1 eggplant, cubed
2 small bell peppers, de-seeded and
coarsely chopped
8 oz tofu, cubed
½ cup tomato purée
1½ cups water
1 lb soba*

Sauce:

1 cup water
4 tsp tamari soy sauce
½ tsp ground ginger
½ tsp Bakon yeast
¼ tsp cayenne pepper
2 Tbsp honey
⅓ cup cider vinegar
2 Tbsp arrowroot powder

Melt the butter in a large, deep skillet. Add the onion and garlic and sauté over low heat for 2 minutes, stirring occasionally. Add the carrot, eggplant, and bell peppers and continue sautéing, stirring occasionally, for 5 minutes. Add the tofu, tomato purée, and water; cover, leaving lid ajar so that some steam can escape. Increase the heat to medium and simmer for 15 minutes, until vegetables are tender and liquid is reduced by half. Whisk all sauce ingredients together. When vegetables are done, add the sauce mixture to the skillet and stir gently for a few moments, until sauce thickens and generously coats the vegetables. Meanwhile, cook soba in boiling, lightly salted water for 5 minutes or until al dente; drain. Turn noodles into a large, shallow bowl or platter and surround with sweet and sour vegetables and tofu. Serve very hot.

* Soba, a traditional Japanese buckwheat noodle, is excellent in this recipe. It can be purchased at an Asian specialty-food store or at some health-food stores. If you can't locate a source, substitute another whole-grain noodle.

Creamy Tofu and Mushrooms

Preparation time: 20 minutes
Makes: 3 to 4 servings
Serve with: cooked egg noodles

  3 Tbsp butter
  2 cups sliced fresh mushrooms
  ½ onion, chopped
  1 large clove garlic, minced
  5 oz tofu, fresh or previously frozen
  ¼ tsp thyme
  1 Tbsp flour
  ½ cup water
  1 Tbsp miso
  1 cup sour cream
  ¼ cup minced fresh parsley
  ½ cup freshly grated Parmesan cheese
    Cooked egg noodles for 4

Melt the butter in a large skillet and sauté the mushrooms, onion, and garlic for 5 minutes. If using fresh tofu, drain, then slice and pat dry with paper towels. If using thawed tofu, squeeze out excess water (tofu will have a sponge-like texture). Crumble tofu into skillet. Add the thyme, and stir for a few moments. Sprinkle the flour over mushroom/tofu mixture. Stir well, then stir the water into the skillet. While sauce thickens, whisk the miso into the sour cream. When sauce in skillet has thickened, stir in sour cream/miso mixture, parsley, and Parmesan cheese. Stir over low heat until heated through. Serve over egg noodles.

For additional tofu recipes, see **Tofu** in the index.

149

FISH AND SEAFOOD MAIN COURSES

Fish and seafood are low in fat, high in complete protein, and easily digestible. Since fresh fish and seafood are abundant in our Pacific Coast location, we have chosen to include them in our diets on an occasional basis. They have a particularly important role to play in the diet of anyone who wants to prepare high quality protein meals quickly.

Most cities have a fish market or a supermarket that prides itself on offering absolutely fresh fish and seafood. Look for such a place, because good flavor and freshness go hand in hand. Check to see that the fish you are choosing is moist and firm. A strong "fishy" odor indicates that a fish is past its prime. Fresh-frozen fish is second-best. If you use it, be sure it is totally thawed so that it cooks evenly.

To retain the naturally sweet and delicate flavor of fish, take care to cook it only until it flakes easily at the gentle touch of a fork. Undercooking is as undesirable with fish and seafood as is overcooking.

Fish is a delicacy, and it requires a delicate hand in the kitchen. Give particular attention to cooking times, and enjoy!

SPECIFIC POINTERS

▶ To **broil** fish, butter the broiler rack and place rinsed and dried fish on the rack about one inch below the heat source. Brush the top with lemon juice and melted butter, if desired. Cook 5—8 minutes on each side, depending on thickness.

▶ To **poach** fish, place it in a skillet and add enough hot water to barely cover it. Season with salt and lemon juice if you wish. Cover the pan and simmer for 5—10 minutes.

▶ To **bake** fish, place it in a buttered baking dish. Dot with butter and sprinkle with herbs if you wish. Bake, uncovered, for 15—25 minutes, depending on thickness, in a 350° oven.

▶ To **barbecue** fish, place it on a buttered grill. Cook over a good-sized moderate fire. Try sprinkling an herb such as thyme or dill on the coals. Turn only when necessary, so that fish will not fall apart. Cook for 5—10 minutes on each side, depending on thickness.

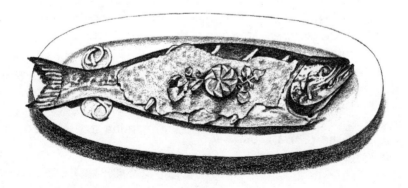

Oyster Crêpes

Ahead of time: prepare crêpes (page 152)
      soften cream cheese to room
      temperature
Preparation time: 10 minutes, then 25
      minutes to bake
Makes: 6 filled crêpes

      4 oz cream cheese, softened
      1 Tbsp lemon juice
      1 Tbsp oyster liquid or water
      1 Tbsp red wine
      6 prepared crêpes
      8 oz fresh or smoked oysters, chopped
      ½ cup sour cream
         Butter
      1 tsp Worcestershire sauce

Preheat oven to 300°. Cream together the cheese, lemon juice, oyster liquid (or water), and wine. Place several small spoonfuls along the center of each crêpe. Top with a layer of oysters and roll. Place the crêpes side by side in a buttered casserole dish. Dot with butter. Mix the sour cream and Worcestershire sauce together and spread on top of the crêpes. Bake, covered, for 20 to 30 minutes.

Crêpe Batter

Preparation time: 10 minutes to prepare
      batter, then 45 minutes to cook
Makes: about 30 crêpes

      6 eggs
      3 cups milk
      3 cups whole wheat pastry flour
      4 Tbsp butter, melted

Beat the eggs in a blender (or with a whisk) until light in color. Add the milk and beat several seconds. Next add the flour and melted butter, a bit at a time, mixing after each addition. Blend until smooth. For even better crêpes, let batter stand at room temperature for one hour before cooking. Cook the crêpes according to the instructions for your crêpe pan. This recipe is good for dinner crêpes as well as for breakfast or dessert crêpes.

This recipe can be cut in half and will still produce excellent results. If you want to cut down on the cooking time, use 2 crêpe pans at once. However this does require trickier timing to prevent burning the crêpes!

Prepared crêpes can be frozen: separate crêpes with layers of waxed paper. Defrost before cooking.

Caper Sauce and Salmon

Preparation time: 15 minutes, then
     1 hour for sauce to chill
Makes: 4 to 6 servings

- ½ cup mayonnaise
- ½ cup sour cream
- 1 Tbsp chopped green onion
- 1 Tbsp chopped parsley
- 1½ Tbsp capers, drained and mashed
- 1½ tsp lemon juice
- 4–6 salmon steaks

Blend together all ingredients except salmon. Cover and chill for at least 1 hour. Broil or poach the salmon, serve, and offer the sauce to be spooned on top. Rock cod or halibut is also good with this sauce.

Poached Fish

Preparation time: 20—25 minutes
Makes: 4 servings

- 4 fish fillets (sole, cod, snapper, etc.)
- 1½ tsp dill weed
     Scant salt and pepper
- 1 pint sour cream
- 2 Tbsp prepared horseradish
- 1–2 Tbsp white wine
- 4 oz chopped olives

Sprinkle the fish with ½ teaspoon of the dill weed, and season with salt and pepper. Roll and secure with a toothpick. Place in a skillet with one inch of hot water. Cover and heat to boiling, reduce to a simmer, and cook for 5—8 minutes or until fish flakes when touched with a fork. Drain and place on a warm serving plate.

Prepare the sauce while the fish is cooking. Whisk the sour cream, horseradish, remaining 1 teaspoon of dill weed, and white wine together in a small saucepan. Heat just to boiling. Pour over cooked fish, top with olives, and serve immediately.

Baked Sole Amandine

Preparation time: 30 minutes
Makes: 2 to 4 servings

- 1 lb petrale sole fillets
- 3 Tbsp butter, melted
- ¼ cup fresh lemon or lime juice
- 1 tsp grated lemon or lime peel
- ½ tsp crushed thyme
- ¼ tsp salt
- ¼ tsp pepper
- ¼ cup slivered almonds
  Fresh chopped parsley

Preheat oven to 450°. Butter the bottom of a shallow baking dish and lay the fish fillets in it. Combine the butter, lemon or lime juice and peel, thyme, salt, and pepper. Pour this over the fish, turning the fish once to coat both sides. Sprinkle with the almonds. Bake for 15—20 minutes, uncovered, until fish flakes when touched with a fork. Garnish with parsley before serving.

Baked Fish in Cream Sauce

Preparation time: 45 minutes
Makes: 3 to 4 servings

- 1 lb fish fillets (any kind)
- 1 Tbsp lemon juice
- ⅛ tsp paprika
- 1 Tbsp butter
- 1 Tbsp flour
- ½ cup milk
- 2 Tbsp white wine
- 1 tsp basil
- ¼ cup bread crumbs
- 1 Tbsp minced parsley
  Lemon wedges

Preheat oven to 350°. If the fillets are large, cut them into serving pieces. Butter a shallow baking dish and arrange the fish on the bottom. Sprinkle with the lemon juice and paprika. In a small saucepan, melt the butter over medium heat. Blend in the flour and stir for a moment, then slowly add the milk. Cook and stir until thick and bubbly. Add the wine and basil and stir. Pour this sauce over the fish. Sprinkle the bread crumbs on top. Bake, uncovered, for 35 minutes. Serve with fresh parsley and lemon wedges.

Red Snapper with Mushroom Topping

Preparation time: 35 minutes
Makes: 2 servings

2	Tbsp butter
⅓	cup chopped onion
6–8	small mushrooms, sliced
1	tsp flour
½	tsp oregano
½	tsp basil
¼	cup sour cream
1	tsp tamari soy sauce
2	tsp lemon juice
2	tsp butter, melted
1	lb red snapper fillets
2	cloves garlic
	Fresh minced parsley

Melt 2 tablespoons butter in a small skillet and sauté the onion and mushrooms until they become limp. Stir in the flour and herbs, mixing until smooth. Add the sour cream, tamari, and lemon juice. Cook for a few minutes until thick and bubbly, stirring occasionally. Remove from heat.

Preheat oven to 350°. Spread 1 teaspoon melted butter in a shallow 1-quart casserole. Lay the fish fillets in a single layer and top with the remaining butter. Using a garlic press, press the garlic cloves over the fish.

Spoon the topping over the fish and bake, covered, for about 20 minutes. Fish is done when it flakes but is still firm. Garnish with parsley before serving.

To serve 4 people, double the ingredient amounts, and bake it in a 2½-quart casserole.

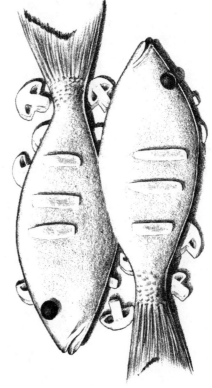

Stove-Top Fish

Preparation time: 25 minutes
Makes: 2 servings

- ¼ cup butter
- 1 medium onion, sliced
- 2 cloves garlic, sliced
- 1 lb snapper, butterfish or cod fillets
- 1 tsp chervil
- 2 tsp minced parsley
- 1 bay leaf
- 1 cup sliced mushrooms
- ½–¾ cup white wine

Melt the butter in a large cast-iron skillet and sauté the onion and garlic until slightly brown. Place the fish on top of the onion and sprinkle with the herbs. Spread the mushrooms on top, then add the wine. Cover the pan and cook over medium heat for about 15 minutes.

Variation: add ⅓ cup sour cream along with the wine.

Stuffed Fish

Preparation time: 15 minutes, then 30 minutes to bake
Makes: 2 servings

- 2 Tbsp olive oil
- 2 green onions, diced
- 1 clove garlic, minced
- ½ tsp tarragon
- ½ tsp basil
- ¼ cup white wine
- ¼ cup lemon juice
- ¼ cup sliced black olives
- ½ cup sour cream
- ½ cup dry bread crumbs
- 2–4 petrale sole fillets or red snapper fillets

Preheat oven to 400°. Heat olive oil in a skillet and sauté the onions and garlic. Stir in the herbs, then add the wine, lemon juice, olives, and sour cream. Heat through. Set aside half the sauce. Mix the bread crumbs with the remaining sauce and place a generous spoonful in the center of each fish fillet. Roll the fish and secure with a toothpick. Place the rolls side by side in a buttered baking dish. Pour the rest of the sauce over the top and bake, covered, for 20 minutes, then uncover and bake an additional 5—10 minutes or until golden brown.

Shrimp Creole

Preparation time: 40 minutes
Makes: 6 servings
Serve with: steamed rice

      3 Tbsp butter
    ½ cup chopped onion
    ½ cup chopped celery
      2 cloves garlic, minced
      1 lb stewed tomatoes
      1 cup tomato sauce
    ½ tsp honey
      1 tsp chili powder
      1 Tbsp Worcestershire sauce
      2 tsp arrowroot powder
      3 cups shrimp*
    ½ cup chopped bell pepper

Melt the butter in a large skillet. Add the onion, celery, and garlic, and cook over medium-low heat until tender. Stir in the tomatoes, tomato sauce, honey, chili powder, and Worcestershire sauce. Simmer, uncovered, for 25 minutes, stirring occasionally. Blend the arrowroot powder with 1 tablespoon of cold water and stir it into sauce. Cook and stir until mixture thickens. Add the shrimp and bell pepper. Cover and simmer about 5 minutes. Serve over hot steamed rice.

* Tiny bay shrimp may be used. If using larger shrimp, remove the shells and de-vein them in advance.

Steamed Clams

Preparation time: 15 minutes
Makes: 2 servings

      2 dozen clams, in their shells
    2½ cups hot water
      4 Tbsp butter
      1 clove garlic, minced

Wash the clams and scrub lightly to remove any dirt. Place in a large pan and cover with the hot water. Steam over medium heat for about 10 minutes, just until they pop open. It is important not to overcook them. While they are steaming, melt the butter in a small pan and blend in the garlic. Serve the clams immediately. Provide the butter for dipping and accompany with French bread and white wine.

Shrimp Curry, Traditional Style

Preparation time: 25 minutes
Makes: 6 servings
Serve with: steamed rice

  6 Tbsp butter
  ½ cup chopped onion
  ½ cup chopped bell pepper
  2 cloves garlic, minced
  1 Tbsp curry powder
  2 tsp lemon juice
  ¼ tsp salt
  ½ tsp ground ginger
  ⅛ tsp chili powder
  2 cups plain yogurt or sour cream
  3 cups shrimp*
    Curry Condiments (page 126)

In a saucepan, melt the butter. Add the onion, bell pepper, and garlic, and sauté over medium heat until just tender. Stir in the curry powder, lemon juice, salt, ginger, and chili powder. Add the yogurt or sour cream and blend well. Stir in the shrimp and cook over low heat just until heated through, about 2 minutes. (Sauce will be thin.)

Serve over steamed rice, with condiments such as chutney, raisins, peanuts, and coconut (see Curry Condiments, page 126).

* You may use tiny bay shrimp. If using larger shrimp, be sure to remove the shells and de-vein them in advance.

Sole Fillets with Capers

Preparation time: 15 minutes to assemble, then 20—30 minutes to bake
Makes: 2 servings

- ½–¾ lb sole fillets
- 2 Tbsp butter
- 3 green onions, chopped
- 1 Tbsp flour
- ¼ cup dry white wine
- ½ cup plain yogurt
- 1 Tbsp minced fresh parsley
- 1 Tbsp capers (not drained)
- 4 large mushrooms, sliced

Preheat oven to 350°. Rinse the fish fillets and place in an oiled baking dish. Melt the butter in a small skillet and sauté the green onions for several minutes. Stir in the flour and cook over low heat for a minute or two. Add the wine and stir, then gradually stir in the yogurt, parsley, and capers. Then add the mushrooms. If the sauce is very thick, add a bit of water. Pour this mixture over the fish. Bake, covered, for 20—30 minutes.

Quick & Simple Scampi

Preparation time: 15 to 20 minutes
Makes: 2 servings
Serve with: steamed rice or bulghur

- 6 Tbsp butter
- ¼ cup minced parsley
- 2 slices onion, finely diced
- 4 large mushrooms, chopped
- 2 large cloves garlic, minced
- ½ tsp anise seeds, crushed
- 16 medium shrimp, peeled and de-veined
- 2 Tbsp white wine
- 1 Tbsp lemon juice

Melt the butter in a saucepan and sauté the parsley, onion, mushrooms, and garlic for 10 minutes. Add the anise and shrimp and cook over medium heat until the shrimp turns pink, about 2 minutes. Remove the shrimp from the pan with a slotted spoon so as not to overcook. Reduce heat to low and stir in the wine and lemon juice. When this is hot, return the shrimp to the pan and reheat for a moment. Serve immediately over steamed rice or bulghur. A true gourmet delight!

Shrimp Oyster Bake

Preparation time: 35 minutes
Makes: 4 servings
Serve with: steamed rice

    1 jar (10 ounces) fresh oysters
    ½ cup chopped onion
    1 cup sliced mushrooms
    3 Tbsp butter
    ½ tsp thyme
       Salt and pepper
    1 Tbsp arrowroot powder
    ½ cup milk
    2 Tbsp white wine
    ½ lb small shrimp
    4 Tbsp grated Parmesan cheese
    2 Tbsp minced parsley

Drain the oysters, reserving the liquid, and cut them into bite-sized pieces. Put them in a small frying pan, pour in the reserved liquid, and cook over medium heat for 5 minutes. Meanwhile, chop the onion and slice the mushrooms. When the oysters are tender, pour them through a colander, again reserving the liquid, and set aside. Place the butter in a frying pan and sauté the onions and mushrooms over low heat until tender. Add the thyme and a little salt and pepper. Stir the mushrooms and onion to the sides of the pan, making a space in the center.

Gradually sprinkle the arrowroot powder into this space, stirring well to blend. Continue to stir and add the milk. Cook for several minutes until thick, stirring occasionally. Pour in the wine and blend. Add the oysters and shrimp. If the sauce is too thick, add a couple of tablespoons of the reserved oyster liquid. Spoon into a small, buttered casserole dish or individual serving dishes. Cover with Parmesan cheese and top with minced parsley. Bake, uncovered, for 5 minutes to heat through and melt the cheese. Serve over steamed rice.

10
BAKED GOODS AND SWEETS

A slice of nut bread or a savory muffin hot from the oven satisfies like nothing else, and the aroma of baking bread or cake makes us feel cozy and well provided for.

You needn't let a busy schedule prevent you from enjoying fresh breads and desserts at home. Many muffins and quick breads, cakes and cookies, and other sweet treats can be assembled in minutes and baked while you relax.

Sweets can be a delightful indulgence all by themselves, or they can be the crowning glory of a meal. When planning a dessert, consider the rest of the meal. Generally speaking, a light dessert is most appropriate after a heavy meal; a rich dessert best follows a lighter meal.

Honey, molasses, and pure maple syrup are always used in our recipes instead of refined sugars, which provide empty calories and may even rob your body of nutrients. Improving the nutritional quality of sweet treats allows us to enjoy them on occasion without hesitation and without guilt!

SPECIFIC POINTERS

▶ For good health's sake, we've developed recipes that use stone-ground whole-grain flours, yet are light and delicious. We use regular whole wheat flour where a grainy texture is desired and whole wheat pastry flour for a finer textured product.

▶ When raw, unfiltered honey has crystallized in the jar, warm it gently until it liquefies. This allows for easier blending with other ingredients.

▶ A rule-of-thumb when converting white flour and white sugar recipes is to substitute equal amounts of whole wheat pastry flour for white, unbleached, or all-purpose flour, and half as much honey for sugar. Honey is always creamed into the wet ingredients before the dry ingredients are added. When honey is used the baking temperature should be lowered about 25°.

▶ Preheat oven and butter your baking pans before assembling a batter or dough, so that the oven is hot when you are ready for it.

▶ Before beginning, let butter soften at room temperature for easier blending (unless it is to be cut in with a pastry cutter, as with biscuits).

▶ A crack down the center of a finished loaf of bread is typical. Don't let it worry you.

▶ Some recipes call for beaten egg whites to lighten the texture and increase rising in baked goods. Bring the whites to room temperature first, and the time it takes to beat them will be decreased.

▶ To test if the bread is done, insert a long toothpick or a bamboo skewer into the center. If it isn't coated with batter when you remove it, the bread is done. Remove bread from the oven and let it cool completely before you slice it. Cooking will continue as the bread cools, achieving the perfect texture.

▶ There are two classic ways to test if a cake is done. One is the same as that described above for breads. The other is to depress the center of the cake gently with a fingertip. If the depression quickly returns to its original position, the cake is done.

▶ Nut breads should be turned out of the pan after baking, to cool on a rack. Store the cooled bread in an airtight container or in foil for at least a day before slicing, to facilitate uncrumbly slicing and to allow the flavor to mellow (that is, of course, if you can wait).

▶ Use only a few strokes when combining flour with wet ingredients in a muffin recipe. Don't worry about a few tiny pockets of unmoistened flour in the batter—an undesirable result of overbeating muffins is a tough and tunneled texture.

Whole Wheat Scones

Preparation time: 25 minutes to assemble,
    then 20 minutes to bake
Makes: 1 dozen

    1   cup buttermilk
    2   Tbsp honey or molasses
    3   cups whole wheat flour
    1   Tbsp baking powder
    ¼   tsp salt
    ⅓   cup butter, melted
    ⅓   cup raisins (or any chopped, dried fruit)

Preheat oven to 400°. Lightly butter a cookie sheet. In a large bowl, beat together the buttermilk and the honey. In another bowl, sift together the flour, baking powder, and salt. Stir any bran left in the sifter back into the flour mixture. Stir half the flour mixture into the buttermilk mixture. Now add the melted butter a little at a time, beating vigorously after each addition. Add the remaining flour mixture and the raisins and mix well; dough should be stiff. Turn dough out onto a floured surface and knead a few minutes. Divide dough into thirds, pat each third out into a thick circle, and quarter each circle with a sharp knife. Place the twelve resulting wedges on a cookie sheet and bake 20 minutes. The scones should be lightly browned. Serve with hot tea, butter, and jams.

166

Oat Raisin Muffins

Preparation time: 10 minutes to assemble,
    then 15—20 minutes to bake
Makes: 1 dozen muffins

    1¼ cups buttermilk (or milk)
    ½   cup rolled oats
    ⅓   cup raisins
    2   cups whole wheat flour
    1   Tbsp baking powder
    1   tsp ground cinnamon
    ½   tsp salt
    2   eggs
    2   Tbsp butter, melted
    3   Tbsp honey
    ⅓   cup chopped nuts
        or sunflower seeds

Preheat oven to 400°. Butter a 12-cup muffin tin. In a large bowl, combine the buttermilk, oats, and raisins and let soak. In a smaller bowl stir together the flour, baking powder, cinnamon, and salt. To buttermilk mixture add the eggs, melted butter, and honey and beat until well blended. Now add flour mixture and stir just until dry ingredients are moistened. Fill buttered muffin tins two-thirds full. Bake for 15—20 minutes or until toothpick inserted in the center comes out clean.

Serve as an accompaniment to soup or stew, or just as a treat.

Banana Bran Muffins

Preparation time: 10 minutes to assemble,
  then 25 minutes to bake
Makes: 10 muffins

       1 cup sifted whole wheat pastry flour
    2½ tsp baking powder
          Pinch of salt
       1 cup bran
       1 Tbsp honey
       2 Tbsp butter, melted
       1 egg
       1 cup mashed ripe (or overripe) banana
       4 Tbsp milk or water

Preheat oven to 400°. Butter 10 cups of a muffin tin. Sift together the flour, baking powder, and salt. Stir in the bran. In another bowl, beat the honey with the melted butter and egg. Add the banana and milk and blend thoroughly. Add the dry ingredients all at once and stir just enough to moisten. Fill buttered muffin cups two-thirds full. Bake for 20—25 minutes.

Bran Muffins

Preparation time: 10 minutes to assemble,
  then 20 minutes to bake
Makes: 1 dozen muffins

       1 cup plus 1 Tbsp whole wheat flour
       1 cup wheat bran
       1 Tbsp baking powder
     ¼ tsp salt
       1 egg
     ¼ cup vegetable oil
     ⅓ cup molasses and/or honey
    1½ cups buttermilk
     ½ cup raisins or
          any dried fruit, chopped

Preheat oven to 400°. Oil a 12-cup muffin tin. Stir together the flour, bran, baking powder, and salt. Whisk the egg with the oil, molasses, buttermilk, and raisins. Add dry ingredients to egg mixture, and beat just until moistened. Fill oiled muffin tins two-thirds full and bake for 20 minutes.

Cheese Dill Muffins

Preparation time: 10 minutes to assemble,
    then 25 minutes to bake
Makes: 10 muffins

1¾ cups whole wheat pastry flour
2½ tsp baking powder
¼ tsp salt
1 cup grated cheddar or jack cheese
1 tsp dill weed
½ tsp crushed caraway seeds
1 egg
1 Tbsp honey
2 Tbsp butter, melted
1 cup milk

Preheat oven to 400°. Butter 10 cups of a muffin tin. Sift together the flour, baking powder, and salt. Stir in the dill and caraway, then stir in the cheese. In another bowl, beat the egg, honey, and melted butter until well blended. Beat in the milk. Add flour mixture and stir just to moisten. Fill buttered muffin cups two-thirds full. Bake for 25—30 minutes.

Cornbread (Corn Muffins)

Preparation time: 20 minutes to assemble,
    then 20—30 minutes to bake
Makes: One 8-inch square pan of
    cornbread, or 12 muffins

1 cup coarse yellow cornmeal
½ cup whole wheat flour
2 tsp baking powder
½ tsp salt
1 egg
3 Tbsp vegetable oil
3 Tbsp honey
1 cup milk or buttermilk (or water)

Preheat oven to 375°. Oil an 8-inch square pan or a 12-cup muffin tin. In a large bowl, stir together the cornmeal, flour, baking powder, and salt. In a smaller bowl, beat the egg with oil and honey until smooth, then add the buttermilk and beat again. Pour wet ingredients into flour mixture and beat vigorously until smooth. Pour mixture into the oiled baking pan and bake for 25—30 minutes; or, if making muffins, fill muffin tins two-thirds full and bake 20 minutes. When a toothpick inserted in the center comes out clean, the cornbread is done. Remove from the oven and let stand in pan for a few minutes. Serve warm or cold.

Biscuits

Preparation time: 15 minutes to assemble, then 15 minutes to bake
Makes: 12 biscuits

- 2 cups sifted whole wheat pastry flour
- 1 Tbsp baking powder
- ½ tsp salt
- ¼ cup cold butter
- ¾ cup milk

Preheat oven to 450°. Butter a cookie sheet. Sift the dry ingredients together into a bowl. Cut in the cold butter with a pastry cutter (or two knives) until the mixture resembles coarse crumbs. Make a well in the center of the flour mixture and pour in the milk all at once. Stir quickly with a fork just until the dough is evenly moistened and beginning to cling together. Turn out onto a lightly floured surface and knead gently, about a dozen strokes. Roll or pat the dough into a half-inch-thick layer. Dip a biscuit cutter or the lip of a water glass into flour, then cut into the dough, pushing straight down to form circles. Place biscuits about three-quarters of an inch apart on a greased cookie sheet and bake for 12—15 minutes. For soft sides, place biscuits close together in a shallow baking pan. For a golden color, brush the tops with milk before baking.

Honey Nut Bread

Preparation time: 15 minutes to assemble, then 60 minutes to bake
Makes: 1 large loaf

- 2 cups whole wheat pastry flour
- 1 tsp salt
- 1 Tbsp baking powder
- 2 eggs, well beaten
- ⅔ cup honey, warmed
- 2 Tbsp butter, melted
- 1 cup buttermilk
- 1 cup chopped nuts
- ½ cup raisins
- Nutmeg

Preheat oven to 325°. Butter the bottom and sides of a large loaf pan. Sift together the flour, salt, and baking powder. Set aside. Whisk the eggs with the honey and butter until well blended. Whisk in the buttermilk. Add the dry ingredients and blend with a wooden spoon until well mixed; fold in the nuts and raisins. Turn into the loaf pan and sprinkle the top with nutmeg. Bake for 50—60 minutes, until the loaf is well browned and a toothpick comes out clean when inserted in the center. Cool in the pan for 10 minutes, then turn out onto a wire rack to finish cooling.

169

Glazed Lemon Bread

Preparation time: 25 minutes to assemble,
    then 40 minutes to bake
Makes: 1 loaf or 1 small bundt cake

    4 Tbsp butter, softened
    ½ cup honey
    2 eggs
    2 tsp grated lemon peel
    2 cups whole wheat pastry flour
 2½ tsp baking powder
    ½ tsp salt
    ¾ cup milk

    Glaze:

    1 Tbsp butter
    2 tsp lemon juice
    2 tsp grated lemon peel
    ¼ cup honey

Preheat oven to 350°. Butter a bundt or loaf pan. Cream together the butter and honey until light and fluffy. Add the eggs and lemon peel, beating until smooth. Set aside. Sift together the flour, baking powder, and salt. Add to the creamed mixture alternately with the milk. Beat until smooth. Pour into the buttered bundt or loaf pan and bake for 30—40 minutes. When a toothpick inserted in the center comes out clean, the loaf is done. Let cool in the pan for 10 minutes, then turn out of the pan onto a serving plate.

Put the glaze ingredients in a small saucepan and heat to the candy point—a rapid boil you cannot stir down. Cook for 1 minute, then cool for 1 minute and pour over the cake. Cool completely, then wrap tightly and refrigerate overnight.

Peggy's Banana-Nut Bread

Ahead of time: soften butter to room
    temperature
Preparation time: 20 minutes to assemble,
    then 1 hour to bake
Makes: 1 large loaf

⅔ cup butter, softened
½ cup honey
2 eggs, beaten
1½ cups ripe (or overripe) bananas,
    mashed
1 tsp baking powder
1 tsp baking soda
½ tsp salt
2¾ cups whole wheat pastry flour
½ cup sour cream or plain yogurt
1 cup chopped nuts

Preheat oven to 350°. Butter a loaf pan. In a
large bowl, cream together the butter and
honey. Add the eggs and bananas and stir
well. In a separate bowl, sift together the
baking powder, baking soda, salt, and
flour. Add the dry ingredients alternately
with sour cream to the creamed mixture,
blending well; fold in the nuts. Spoon into
the buttered loaf pan. Bake for 60 minutes.
Cool for 24 hours in the pan (if you can wait
that long).

Cranberry Orange Nut Bread

Preparation time: 15 minutes to assemble,
    then 1 hour to bake
Makes: 1 loaf

2 cups whole wheat pastry flour
1½ tsp baking powder
½ tsp baking soda
¼ tsp salt
¼ cup cold butter
¾ cup orange juice
1 Tbsp grated orange rind
1 egg, well beaten
¾ cup honey, warmed
½ cup chopped nuts
2 cups fresh whole cranberries

Preheat oven to 350°. Butter a loaf pan. Sift
together the flour, baking powder, baking
soda, and salt. Cut in the butter until mixture resembles coarse cornmeal. Beat together the orange juice and rind, egg, and
honey. Pour all at once into dry ingredients,
stirring just enough to moisten. Fold in the
nuts and berries. Spoon into the buttered
loaf pan and bake for 1 hour, or until knife
blade inserted in center comes out clean.
A wonderfully festive bread!

171

Zucchini Bread

Preparation time: 20 minutes, then 1 hour
    to bake
Makes: 2 loaves

    3 eggs
    1 cup oil
1¼ cups honey
    2 cups peeled, grated zucchini
    2 tsp vanilla extract
    3 cups whole wheat pastry flour
    1 tsp baking soda
¼ tsp baking powder
    1 tsp salt
    1 Tbsp cinnamon
½ cup chopped nuts (optional)

Preheat oven to 325°. Butter two loaf pans. Beat eggs until light and foamy. Beat in the oil, honey, zucchini, and vanilla extract. In a separate bowl, stir together the flour, baking soda, baking powder, salt, and cinnamon. Add the flour mixture and blend well. Add the nuts. Spoon into loaf pans and bake for 1 hour, or until a knife blade inserted in the center comes out clean. Remove from pans at once and let cool on a rack.

Carrot Cake

Preparation time: 30 minutes to assemble,
    then 45 minutes to bake
Makes: one 9 x 13-inch cake

1½ cups oil
1½ cups honey
    2 tsp vanilla
    4 eggs
    2 cups whole wheat pastry flour
    4 tsp baking powder
    2 tsp cinnamon
    3 cups grated carrots
    1 cup chopped walnuts or pecans
      Cream Cheese Frosting (p 177) optional

Preheat oven to 350°. Butter a 9 x 13-inch cake pan. Whisk together the oil and honey; add the vanilla. Add the eggs one at a time, whisking after each addition. In a separate bowl, sift together the dry ingredients. Add the dry ingredients and the carrots to the honey/oil mixture and stir. Fold in the chopped nuts. Turn into the buttered cake pan and bake for 45-50 minutes.

This cake can also be baked in two 9-inch round cake pans. Bake for 35 minutes at 375°. This is delicious as is; it is even richer frosted with Cream Cheese Frosting.

Orange Bundt Cake

Preparation time: 20 minutes to assemble,
    then 30 minutes to bake
Makes: 1 small bundt cake
    or one 9 x 9-inch cake

2 cups whole wheat pastry flour
½ tsp salt
1 Tbsp baking powder

2 eggs, beaten
½ cup orange juice
½ cup honey, warmed
¼ cup butter, melted
1 tsp vanilla

Topping:

1 Tbsp butter
2 tsp grated orange rind
¼ cup honey
1 tsp cinnamon
Dash of nutmeg

Preheat oven to 400°. Butter the baking dish. In a large bowl, sift together the dry ingredients. In a separate bowl, blend together the eggs, orange juice, honey, melted butter, and vanilla. Pour into the flour mixture, stirring just to blend. Pour into a buttered bundt or 9 x 9-inch pan. Bake for 30—35 minutes (depending on the pan you use). Cool for 15 minutes before removing from the pan. This cake is delicious as is, and even more wonderful with the orange glaze topping.

Topping: melt the butter in a small saucepan and add the orange rind, honey, cinnamon, and nutmeg. Heat rapidly to the candy point—a very rapid boil you cannot stir down. Cook for 1 minute. Remove from the heat and stir. Cool for a few moments, then pour over the cake.

173

Applesauce Cake

Preparation time: 15 minutes to assemble,
    then 60 minutes to bake
Makes: one 9-inch square cake or 1 small
    bundt cake

    2 cups whole wheat pastry flour
    2 tsp baking powder
    ½ tsp cloves
    ½ tsp cinnamon
    ½ cup butter
    ½ cup honey
    2 eggs, beaten
  1½ cups applesauce

Preheat oven to 350°. Butter the baking
pan. Sift together the flour, baking powder, cloves, and cinnamon, and set aside.
Cream the butter and honey together, then
stir in the eggs. Stir in the applesauce. Add
to the flour mixture and mix together until
well combined. Pour into the pan and bake
60—70 minutes, or until a toothpick inserted in the center comes out clean.

Chocolate Swirl Cake

Preparation time: 15 minutes to assemble,
    then 30 minutes to bake
Makes: 1 small bundt cake or a 9 x 9-inch
    cake

    ½ cup butter, softened
    ½ cup honey
    2 eggs, beaten
  1½ cups flour
    ¾ tsp salt
    2 tsp baking powder
    ⅔ cup milk
    ⅓ cup powdered cocoa

Preheat oven to 350°. Butter the baking
pan. Cream together the butter and
honey. Add the eggs and beat until light
and fluffy. In a separate bowl, sift together
the flour, salt, and baking powder. Add this
to the creamed mixture alternately with the
milk, beating well after each addition.
Spoon half of the batter into the baking
pan. Sprinkle the cocoa over the batter.
Add remaining batter. Insert a knife verti-
cally and stir to produce swirl. Bake 35
minutes, or until a toothpick inserted in the
center comes out clean. Cool for 5 minutes,
then turn out of the pan onto a serving dish.

Strawberry Glazed Cake

Ahead of time: soften butter to room
    temperature
Preparation time: 15 minutes to assemble,
    then 35—40 minutes to bake
Makes: 1 small bundt cake
    or one 9 x 9-inch cake

   1 cup butter, softened
   1 cup honey
   4 eggs
   3 cups whole wheat pastry flour
   1 tsp salt
   4 tsp baking powder
1⅓ cups milk

   Glaze:

   2 Tbsp butter
  ¼ cup honey
   2 Tbsp strawberry juice
   2 Tbsp strawberry pulp

Preheat oven to 350°. Butter the baking dish. In a large bowl, cream together the butter and honey. Add the eggs and beat until light and fluffy. In a separate bowl, sift together the flour, salt, and baking powder. Add this to the creamed mixture alternately with the milk, beating well after each addition. Spoon into the buttered bundt or cake pan. Bake for 35—40 minutes or until a toothpick inserted in the center comes out clean. Cool for 5 minutes, then turn out of the pan onto a serving dish.

Put the glaze ingredients into a small saucepan. Heat to the candy point—a very rapid boil you cannot stir down. Cook for 1 minute. Remove from heat and stir. Cool for a few moments, then pour over the cake.

If you have extra strawberries, arrange them around the edge of the serving plate, or fill the center of the bundt cake with sliced strawberries before serving. This cake is extremely rich, so serve thin slices.

Spice Cake

Preparation time: 15 minutes to assemble,
    then 30 minutes to bake
Makes: 1 small bundt cake
    or one 8 x 8-inch cake

2⅓ cups whole wheat pastry flour
  1 tsp salt
  2 tsp baking powder
1½ tsp cinnamon
  1 tsp nutmeg
  ⅔ cup butter, softened
  ¾ cup honey
  1 cup buttermilk
  3 eggs, beaten

    Topping:
  1 Tbsp butter
  ¼ cup honey
  2 Tbsp buttermilk
    Nutmeg
    Cinnamon
  ¼ cup finely chopped nuts

Preheat oven to 350°. Butter the baking pan. Sift the flour, salt, baking powder, cinnamon, and nutmeg into a small bowl. In a larger bowl, cream together the butter and honey. Add the buttermilk and eggs, mixing well to blend. Pour in the dry ingredients and stir just to moisten. Spoon into

the baking pan and bake for 30—35 minutes or until a toothpick comes out clean. Cool for 10 minutes, then turn out onto a serving plate.

In a small saucepan, combine all topping ingredients except the nuts. Heat to the candy point—a rapid boil you cannot stir down. Cook for 1 minute, then add the nuts. Cool for a few moments and then pour over the cake.

Carob Frosting

Preparation time: 10 minutes
Makes: 1½ cups

  ½ cup whipping cream
  ¼ cup honey, warmed
  2 Tbsp sesame oil
  1 tsp vanilla extract
  ⅓ cup carob powder
  ⅔ cup dry powdered milk (non-instant)

Whisk together the whipping cream, honey, sesame oil, and vanilla extract until well combined. Stir in the carob powder and the dry milk and beat until creamy and smooth.

Cream Cheese Frosting

Ahead of time: soften cream cheese
    to room temperature
Preparation time: 15 minutes
Makes: 1½ cups

  8 oz cream cheese, softened
  2 Tbsp honey
  1 tsp vanilla extract
  ½ cup whipping cream

Blend the cream cheese, honey, and vanilla until smooth. Add the whipping cream a little at a time, beating vigorously until perfectly combined.

Variation: add 2 teaspoons of grated lemon or orange rind or 1 teaspoon ground cinnamon.

Whipped Cream

Preparation time: 5 minutes
Makes: 2 cups

  1 cup well-chilled whipping cream
  ½ tsp honey, warmed
  ⅛ tsp vanilla extract

In a deep bowl, beat the cream with an eggbeater or electric mixer until it is fairly thick. Add the honey and vanilla and continue beating until cream is stiff enough to form soft peaks when beaters are removed.

Variation: at the end add a scant teaspoon of grated lemon or orange rind or a pinch of nutmeg or cinnamon.

Butterscotch Brownies

Preparation time: 10 minutes to assemble,
   then 30 minutes to bake
Makes: 16 brownies

   ¼ cup oil
   1 Tbsp molasses
   ¾ cup honey, warmed
   2 eggs, beaten
   2 tsp vanilla extract
   1 cup wheat germ
   ¼ tsp salt
   ½ cup milk powder
   ½ tsp baking powder
   ½ cup chopped walnuts

Preheat oven to 350°. Butter one 8 x 8-inch baking pan. Stir together the oil, molasses, and honey. Mix in the eggs, vanilla, wheat germ, and salt, and stir just to moisten. Sift in the milk powder and baking powder, stirring again just to moisten. Fold in the walnuts. Turn into the pan and bake for 30 minutes.

Brownies

Preparation time: 15 minutes to assemble,
   then 25 minutes to bake
Makes: 16 brownies

   ⅔ cup unbleached white flour
   ⅓ cup cocoa (or carob) powder
   ½ tsp baking powder
   ½ tsp salt
   2 eggs
   1 tsp vanilla
   ⅓ cup oil
   ⅔ cup honey
   1 cup chopped nuts

Preheat oven to 350°. Butter an 8 x 8-inch baking pan. Sift together the flour, cocoa (or carob), baking powder, and salt into a small bowl, and set aside. In a larger bowl, slightly beat the eggs and whisk in the vanilla, oil, and honey. Mix until smooth. Stir in the flour mixture and nuts, blending until smooth. Pour into the pan. Arrange additional walnut halves on top if desired. Bake for 25—30 minutes. Allow to cool about one hour before cutting. Serve alone or with vanilla ice cream or whipped cream.

English Baked Custard

Ahead of time: bring eggs to room
    temperature
Preparation time: 15 minutes to assemble,
    then 45 minutes to bake
Makes: one 8-inch pie or 6 custard cups

    4 eggs, room temperature
    ¼ cup honey, warmed
    ½ tsp salt
  2½ cups milk, scalded
    1 tsp vanilla extract
    ¼ tsp nutmeg

Preheat oven to 325°. Gently whisk together
the eggs, then whisk in the honey until well
combined. Gently stir in the salt, scalded
milk, and vanilla. Continue to stir until well
blended, but try not to make bubbles, as
this will produce a grainy texture. Pour into
an 8-inch pie crust or 6 individual ramekins.
Sprinkle nutmeg on top. Place ramekins in a
shallow baking pan containing an inch of
warm water. Bake on the middle rack of the
oven for 45 minutes or until a knife inserted
into the custard comes out clean. Remove
from the oven and allow the custard to cool
in the pan of water, then refrigerate until
serving time.

Serve as is, or topped with honey, jam, fruit,
or a liqueur. The secrets to perfect custard
are to have the ingredients at room temperature, and to have an evenly preheated
oven.

Fruit Crisp

Preparation time: 10 minutes to assemble,
    then 35 minutes to bake
Makes: one 8 x 8-inch pan or one pie

6–8 peaches, pears, or apples
    Juice of 1 lemon (with apples only)
    Pinch nutmeg
    Dash cinnamon
  ½ cup honey, warmed
  1 cup whole wheat flour
  ½ cup cold butter

Preheat oven to 375°. Butter an 8 x 8-inch
baking dish, or one pie pan. Wash, quarter,
core, and slice the fruit and place in the
baking dish. If using apples, add lemon
juice and toss. Drizzle the warm honey over
the fruit and sprinkle with nutmeg and
cinnamon. In a small bowl, use a pastry
cutter or two knives to cut the butter into
the flour to the size of small peas. Toss this
mixture over the fruit. Bake for 45 minutes.
This is a Father's Day special!

179

Fruit Cobbler

Preparation time: 15 minutes to assemble,
    then 30 minutes to bake
Makes: one 9 x 9-inch cobbler

    Fresh or canned fruit*
    Cinnamon, nutmeg (optional)
1–4 Tbsp honey, warmed (amount will vary
    with sweetness of fruit used)
  1 cup whole wheat pastry flour
1½ tsp baking powder
  ½ tsp salt
  ¼ cup cold butter
  1 egg, beaten
  ⅓ cup milk

Preheat oven to 350°. Butter the bottom and sides of a 9 x 9-inch baking dish. Fill almost to the top with fruit. Drizzle with honey. Fruits such as apples, pears, or pineapple are excellent with cinnamon and nutmeg sprinkled on them.

Combine flour, baking powder, and salt in a bowl. Cut in the butter. Stir in the egg and milk. If batter isn't spreadable, add a bit more milk to achieve a thick but spreadable consistency. Dot the top of the fruit with teaspoons of the batter, spreading to make a thin layer. Bake for 30 minutes.

* Amount varies, depending on type of fruit: for peaches, apples, or pears, you need 6 to 8 whole fresh fruits or 1 to 2 quarts canned fruits. Berries or cherries are good, too.

Peaches Flambé

Preparation time: about 5 minutes
Serve in a heatproof bowl

> Canned peach halves
> Brandy

Arrange the drained peach halves, cut side down, in a serving dish and pour a small amount of brandy over them. Warm another tablespoonful of brandy over a flame, then light it with a match and pour over the peaches. This should be done at the table, as the flambé is exciting to watch. You may want to practice once before you perform for guests.

The peaches are tasty served as is, or with whipped cream.

Cherries Jubilee

Preparation time: 10—12 minutes
Makes: 4 servings

> 1 qt canned cherries
> ¼ cup honey
> 2 Tbsp cherry liquid
> 1 tsp cornstarch
> 1 Tbsp cold water
> ¼ cup Kirsch,™ or brandy, warmed

Place cherries, honey, and cherry liquid in a saucepan and simmer over low heat for 8 minutes. Lift out the cherries with a slotted spoon and set aside. In a small jar, shake the cornstarch with the cold water. Stir into the syrup and cook over low heat until smooth and translucent. Add the cherries and stir until heated. At this point transfer to a serving bowl, then pour the warmed Kirsch,™ or brandy over the cherries and light with a match.

181

Papaya Compote

Preparation time: 10 minutes
Mix in a pretty bowl.

2–3 papayas, cubed
  1 pineapple, cubed
  2 bananas, sliced
  ⅓ cup dry white wine

Toss together equal parts of papaya and pineapple, with banana slices. Pour the wine over the fruit; cover and refrigerate several hours. Toss gently before serving.

Simple Fruit and Cheese Dessert

Preparation time: 10 minutes
Makes: 4 servings

  4 tsp pure maple syrup
  2 Tbsp raisins
  1 pt ricotta cheese
    Dash cinnamon
    Fresh fruit for 4 servings (apple, peach, or banana slices—or a combination of these)

Stir the syrup and raisins into the ricotta until well combined. Divide this mixture among 4 dessert dishes; sprinkle lightly with cinnamon and surround with fresh fruit. A mint leaf garnish is a refreshing touch.

Chocolate Chip Cookies

Ahead of time: soften butter to room temperature
Preparation time: 15 minutes to assemble, then 10 minutes to bake
Makes: 3 to 4 dozen

2¾ cups whole wheat pastry flour
  2 tsp baking powder
  1 tsp salt
  1 cup butter, softened
  1 cup honey
  1 tsp vanilla extract
  ½ tsp water
  2 eggs
  2 cups chocolate chips (or carob chips)
  1 cup chopped nuts

Preheat oven to 375°. Butter a cookie sheet. Sift together the flour, baking powder, and salt. In a separate bowl, cream together the butter, honey, vanilla, and water. Beat until creamy, then beat in the eggs, mixing well. Add the flour mixture and combine until well blended—the batter will be stiff. Stir in the chocolate chips and nuts. Drop by teaspoonsful onto the cookie sheet and bake for 10—12 minutes.

Saucy Ginger Cookies

Ahead of time: soften butter to room
    temperature
Preparation time: 15 minutes to assemble,
    then 10 minutes to bake
Makes: 4 to 5 dozen

    1 cup butter, softened
    1 cup honey
    1 egg
    ½ cup molasses
    4 cups whole wheat pastry flour
    4 tsp baking powder
 1½ tsp cinnamon
 1½ tsp powdered ginger
    ½ tsp ground cloves
    ¼ tsp salt
    2 cups applesauce

Preheat oven to 350°. Butter a cookie
sheet. Cream together the butter and
honey; blend in the egg and molasses. In a
separate bowl, sift together the flour, baking powder, spices, and salt. Add flour
mixture and applesauce alternately to the
butter/honey mixture. Combine well. Drop
by teaspoonsful onto the cookie sheet.
Bake for 8—10 minutes.

Thumbprint Cookies

Ahead of time: soften butter to room
    temperature
Preparation time: 15 minutes to assemble,
    then 13 minutes to bake
Makes: 2 dozen

    ½ cup butter, softened
    ¼ cup honey
    1 egg, separated
    ½ tsp vanilla extract
    1 cup sifted unbleached flour
    ¼ tsp salt
    ¾ cup ground walnuts
        Jam

Preheat oven to 375°. Cream together the
butter and honey. Blend in the egg yolk and
vanilla and mix thoroughly. Sift in the flour
and salt and mix well. Lightly beat the egg
white in a separate bowl. Roll into 1-inch
balls and dip in the egg white. Roll in the
ground nuts. Place one inch apart on an
ungreased cookie sheet. Bake for 5
minutes. Remove from oven and quickly
press in the center of each cookie with a
spoon. Return to the oven and bake 8
minutes longer. Cool on a rack. Place about
¼ teaspoon of jam in center of each cookie.

Tahini Cookies

Preparation time: 15 minutes to assemble,
   then 15 minutes to bake
Makes: 2½ dozen

   1½ cups whole wheat flour
    1 tsp baking powder
    1 tsp Chinese 5-spice (page 32)
       Dash of salt
    2 eggs
    1 tsp vanilla
    ¼ cup oil
    2 Tbsp honey
    1 Tbsp molasses
    ½ cup tahini
    ½ cup raisins

Preheat oven to 350°. Butter a cookie sheet. Sift together the flour, baking powder, 5-spice, and salt into a small bowl. Stir any wheat bran that remains in the sifter back into the flour mixture. In a large bowl, beat the eggs with the vanilla, oil, honey, and molasses; then beat in the tahini. Combine tahini mixture with flour mixture and beat until smooth. Stir in the raisins. Drop by rounded teaspoonsful onto the cookie sheet and bake for 15 minutes.

Peanut-Oatmeal Cookies

Ahead of time: soften butter to room
   temperature
Preparation time: 10 minutes to assemble,
   then 15 minutes to bake
Makes: 2½ dozen

    ½ cup butter, softened
    1 egg
    ½ cup pure maple syrup
    ½ cup peanut butter
    1 tsp vanilla extract
   1½ cups whole wheat pastry flour
    1 tsp baking powder
    ½ tsp sea salt
    1 cup rolled oats
    ½ cup raisins

Preheat oven to 350°. Beat together the butter, egg, syrup, peanut butter, and vanilla until smooth and creamy. In a separate bowl, stir the flour with the baking powder and salt; then add this to the creamy mixture a third at a time, beating until smooth after each addition. Stir in the oats and raisins. Drop by rounded teaspoonsful onto an ungreased cookie sheet. Bake for 12—15 minutes.

Peanut Banana Morsels

Ahead of time: soften butter to room
    temperature
Preparation time: 15 minutes to assemble,
    then 12 minutes to bake
Makes: 1½ dozen

     1 cup plus 1 Tbsp whole wheat flour
     2 tsp baking powder
    ¼ tsp salt
    ¼ cup butter, softened
    ½ cup peanut butter
    ¼ cup honey
     1 tsp vanilla extract
     1 egg
     1 medium banana

Preheat oven to 350°. Sift the flour with the
baking powder and salt into a small bowl.
Stir any bran flakes that remain in the sifter
back into the flour mixture. In a larger bowl,
cream together the softened butter and the
peanut butter until smooth and perfectly
blended. Now add the honey, vanilla, and
egg and beat vigorously until the mixture is
smooth once again. Pour the flour mixture
into the peanut butter mixture and stir until
well blended. Cut the banana into nine
thick slices, then cut each of the slices in
half. Flour your hands and pick up about a
tablespoonful of dough and wrap it around
a chunk of banana so that the banana is
completely sealed in. Place on an ungreased cookie sheet. Bake for 12 minutes;
cool on a wire rack.

Peanut Butter Cookies

Ahead of time: soften butter to room
    temperature
Preparation time: 15 minutes to assemble,
    then 10 minutes to bake
Makes: 4 dozen

    ½ cup butter, softened
    ½ cup peanut butter
    ¾ cup honey
     1 egg, beaten
    ½ tsp vanilla extract
    1½ cups whole wheat pastry flour
    1½ tsp baking powder
    ¼ tsp salt

Preheat oven to 375°. Cream together the
butter, peanut butter, and honey. Blend in
the egg and vanilla. Sift in the flour, baking
powder, and salt; stir well—batter will be
stiff. Shape into 1-inch balls and place 2
inches apart on an ungreased cookie sheet.
Press with a fork into a crisscross pattern.
Bake for 10 minutes.

11
MORNING MEALS

Your first meal of the day is an important one. The body has been without food for many hours and needs to be well nourished. Don't force yourself to eat immediately upon arising; but, when you do get hungry, eat a well-balanced meal. Including fruit, protein, and a complex carbohydrate (such as cereal grains or whole-grain bread) will insure that you maintain a consistent energy level until your next meal.

Brunch is fast becoming a favorite weekend pastime. It's a perfect meal to prepare without fuss, and to share with friends.

The recipes in this section range from a hearty peasant porridge to sophisticated poached-egg dishes and omelettes. Take your pick, and make your morning meal a special one.

SPECIFIC POINTERS

▶ To make light and fluffy pancakes or waffles, first add the yolks to the batter, then fold in the beaten egg whites just before cooking.

▶ Pancakes should be cooked over low to medium heat until bubbles form and burst on the exposed side, leaving tiny craters. Flip over and bake for about one minute longer.

▶ Waffle cooking instructions vary, depending on your waffle iron.

▶ **Egg cooking techniques:**

Fried eggs: In a cast-iron skillet, melt a small amount of butter over medium heat. Drop in the eggs and season with salt, pepper, and/or herbs if desired. When the whites are set and the edges cooked, add ½ teaspoon of water per egg to the center of the pan. Cover tightly and continue cooking over low heat until the eggs are cooked to your liking. This method steams the yolks so the eggs needn't be turned.

Poached eggs: Heat 3—4 inches of water in a saucepan or frying pan. When the water is almost boiling, add a couple of tablespoonsful of white or cider vinegar and stir. Carefully break the eggs into the swirling water, keeping the water moving by gently stirring, if necessary; otherwise the eggs will stick. Cook over low heat for 3—5 minutes, until the whites are firm. Remove the eggs with a slotted spoon, being careful not to break them, and drain for a moment before slipping them onto plates.

Soft or hard-boiled eggs: Place eggs in a saucepan and cover with cold water to a level at least one inch above the eggs. Bring to a rapid boil. Reduce to a gentle boil and cook 2—4 minutes for soft-boiled eggs and 8—10 minutes for hard-boiled eggs. Cool briefly under cold running water, and serve at once. If the hard-boiled eggs are intended for later use, let them cool completely in a pan, then refrigerate until needed.

Scrambled eggs: Beat eggs with a small amount of milk. Season with salt and pepper if you wish. Melt 1 tablespoon butter in a skillet. Pour in egg mixture and turn heat down to low. Do not disturb until the eggs just begin to set. Then begin to scramble by lifting and stirring gently until the eggs are cooked the way you like them.

Omelettes: For one large omelette, beat 2 or 3 eggs with a small amount of milk, and salt or tamari soy sauce and pepper if you wish. Melt 2 tablespoons butter in a cast-iron skillet or omelette pan over moderate heat and tilt the pan so the butter coats the bottom evenly. When the pan is hot enough to make a drop of water sizzle, pour in the egg mixture. Tip pan to cover bottom with the egg mixture. In a minute or two, when eggs begin to set, gently lift the cooked edges away from the pan and let the uncooked portion run to the bottom. Continue this process until eggs are almost set, then add desired filling on one side and gently fold the other side over it. Let the filling heat for a minute or two, then slide the omelette onto a plate. Be sure to use ample butter, and add more butter before cooking each subsequent omelette.

Soft-Boiled Eggs
with Toast Fingers

Preparation time: 10 minutes
Makes: 2 to 4 servings

  4 eggs
  4 slices whole wheat toast
     Butter

Place the eggs in a saucepan and cover with cold water to a level at least 1 inch above the eggs. Bring to a rapid boil; reduce heat, and gently cook 2—4 minutes, depending on how you like them. While they are cooking, make the toast and butter it. Cut each slice into about ¾-inch "fingers" and serve alongside the prepared eggs. Serve in egg cups, if you have them, or shell the eggs and serve in a bowl. The toast "fingers" are to be dipped into the yolk.

This recipe will serve two to four people, depending on their appetites, and it is easily doubled. Serve fresh orange slices alongside, to round out the meal.

Poached Eggs
with Parmesan Cheese

Preparation time: 10 minutes
Makes: 2 to 4 servings

  4 eggs
  2 English muffins, halved
  4 Tbsp freshly grated Parmesan cheese
     Butter
     Fresh tomato slices

Poach the eggs according to the instructions given above under "Egg cooking techniques" in the **Specific Pointers** section. While the eggs are cooking, toast the English muffins and butter them generously. When the eggs are cooked, gently lift them from the water with a slotted spoon. Drain a moment, then place an egg on each muffin half. Immediately sprinkle with Parmesan cheese. Serve with a couple of slices of fresh tomato alongside.

This recipe will serve two to four people, depending on their appetites. It is best to poach only 4 eggs at a time—if they are crowded together, they tend to cook unevenly.

Poached Eggs "Benedict" Style

Preparation time: 20 minutes
Makes: 4 to 8 servings*

    8 eggs
    4 English muffins, halved
    1 medium avocado, sliced
       Hollandaise Sauce (page 92)

Prepare the Hollandaise Sauce and place it in a double boiler, or on the back of the stove to keep warm. Poach the eggs according to the instructions given under "Egg cooking techniques" in the **Specific Pointers** section. While the eggs are cooking, toast and butter the four English muffin halves and place a couple of slices of avocado on each. When the eggs are cooked, gently lift them from the water with a slotted spoon. Drain a moment, then place one on each muffin. Smother with Hollandaise sauce and serve immediately.

* Ingredients are given for 4 to 8 servings because the recipe for Hollandaise Sauce is enough for that many servings.

Poached Eggs with Cheese and Avocado

Preparation time: 10 minutes
Makes: 2 to 4 servings

    4 eggs
    2 English muffins, halved
       Butter
       Cheese slices to cover muffins
    ½ medium tomato, thinly sliced
    ½ medium avocado, thinly sliced
    4 Tbsp sour cream
       Dijon Sour Cream Sauce (page 90)
       optional
       Salsa (page 94) , optional

Poach the eggs according to "Egg Cooking Techniques" in the **Specific Pointers** section. While the eggs are cooking, toast the muffin halves and butter them generously. Place a couple of slices of cheese on each hot muffin, and top with the tomato and avocado slices. When the eggs are cooked, gently lift them from the water with a slotted spoon. Drain for a moment, then place one on each muffin. Top with a tablespoonful of sour cream, Dijon Sour Cream Sauce, or fresh Salsa.

191

Baked Eggs

Preparation time: 10 minutes to assemble, then 20 minutes to bake
Makes: 4 servings

      Butter
  6 eggs
  1 cup milk
      Salt
      Cayenne pepper

Preheat oven to 350°. Butter a pie plate or similar size baking dish. Separate the eggs. With an eggbeater or electric mixer, whip the egg whites until they are thick enough to form soft peaks when you lift out the beaters.

Whisk the egg yolks with the milk, ½ teaspoon salt, and a few shakes of cayenne pepper. Slowly fold the beaten whites into the yolk mixture until smooth and well blended. Pour into the baking dish and bake for 20 minutes. These eggs are like meringue and are perfect with biscuits or muffins smothered in a creamy sauce.

Scrambled Eggs with Onions

Preparation time: 15 minutes
Makes: 4 servings

  1 bunch green onions
  2 Tbsp butter
6–8 eggs
  2 Tbsp milk
  ¼ cup grated Parmesan cheese
  ¼ tsp salt
      Dash cayenne pepper

Trim, wash, and chop the green onions, discarding most of the green portion. Melt 2 tablespoons butter in a large cast-iron skillet. Add the onions and sauté over medium heat, stirring frequently. Beat the eggs with the milk, Parmesan cheese, salt, and pepper. When onions become limp, pour in the eggs. Let them cook for a minute or two without stirring, then gently lift and fold until eggs are cooked to your liking. Serve very hot with buttered toast and fresh fruit.

Asparagus and Cheese Omelette

Preparation time: 20 minutes
Makes: 2 servings

  8 slender asparagus stalks (young and
      tender)
  2 Tbsp butter
  2 Tbsp minced or grated onion
 ½ tsp tarragon
  5 eggs
  1 Tbsp milk
 ¼ tsp salt
      Freshly ground black pepper
 ½ cup grated Swiss cheese

Wash the asparagus and trim off any tough ends. Slice the asparagus on a slant into one-inch pieces. Melt 1 tablespoon butter in a small pan and add the onion, asparagus, and tarragon to it. Sauté over low heat, stirring occasionally, while you follow the rest of the recipe instructions. Beat the eggs with the milk, salt, and a few grinds of black pepper. Melt the remaining tablespoon butter over medium heat in a large omelette pan or cast-iron skillet. Pour in the eggs and let cook for 2 minutes or until set on the bottom. Now begin lifting the cooked edges away from the pan to allow the uncooked portion to run underneath.

Continue this procedure until egg is almost all set. Now arrange the asparagus mixture on half the omelette, top with grated cheese, and fold the other half over. Leave in the pan for a minute longer to melt cheese, then slide out onto a serving plate. Share and enjoy!

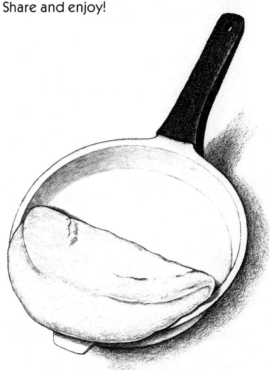

Hash Browned Potatoes

Preparation time: 30 minutes
Makes: 4 to 6 servings

> 4 large potatoes
> 6 Tbsp butter
> Salt
> Pepper
> Onions, sliced (optional)

Place a large pot on the stove with about 4 quarts of water in it. Cover and bring to a rapid boil. Scrub and cut the potatoes into ½-inch cubes. Drop into the rapidly boiling water. Add about ½ teaspoon salt and cook until just tender, about 5 minutes. Drain completely in a colander (about 10 minutes). (Or cook the potatoes the night before and refrigerate until morning.) Place 4 tablespoons of butter in a large cast-iron frying pan and melt over medium-high heat, but be careful not to scorch the butter. Add the potatoes and spread out to cover the bottom of the pan. (It's alright if some of them don't touch the pan.) Fry the potatoes for several minutes, then use a large spatula to turn them. Continue cooking until well browned, adding the additional butter about halfway through the cooking time. When they are crisp and well browned, season with salt and freshly ground black pepper. Serve steaming hot with your favorite eggs. If you like onions, sauté some slices for a few minutes in the butter before adding the potatoes.

Orange Whole Wheat Pancakes

Preparation time: 25 minutes
Makes: 4 servings

> 2 cups whole wheat pastry flour
> 1 tsp baking powder
> ½ tsp salt
> 2 eggs
> ¼ cup butter, melted
> 1½ cups orange juice
> ½ cup finely chopped nuts (optional)

Sift together the flour, baking powder, and salt. Beat the eggs with butter. Add half the flour mixture to the egg mixture and beat, then add half the orange juice and beat again, then add remainder of flour and beat again. Now add enough additional orange juice to make a slightly thick batter. Fry on hot buttered griddle or skillet. Serve with fruit topping or butter and pure maple syrup.

194

Apple Nut Pancakes

Preparation time: 20 minutes
Makes: about ten 4-inch pancakes*

 1 cup whole wheat flour
1½ tsp baking powder
    Pinch of salt
 2 eggs, separated
 ¼ cup vegetable oil
 1 Tbsp honey
 ½ cup apple juice
 ½ cup yogurt (or buttermilk)
 ¼ cup coarsely chopped walnuts
    Pure maple syrup

Sift the flour, baking powder, and salt together into a small bowl. Stir any bran
remaining in the sifter back into the mixture.
In a large bowl, beat the egg yolks with the
oil, honey, apple juice, and yogurt until very
well blended. Stir in the nuts, then flour
mixture, until just blended. Beat the egg
whites with an eggbeater or electric mixer
until peaks form when you lift beaters out.
Fold egg whites into batter. Fry on hot,
lightly buttered griddle or pan.

 * Recipe may easily be doubled, if desired.

Zucchini Pancakes

Preparation time: 15 minutes
Makes: 4 servings

 2 tsp salt
 4 cups grated zucchini
 3 eggs
 1 cup whole wheat pastry flour
 1 tsp curry powder
 2 tsp baking powder
 ½ cup milk
    Butter

In a shallow bowl, sprinkle the zucchini with
the salt and set aside for 10 minutes. Drain
well in a colander, pressing out the excess
liquid. Beat the eggs in a small bowl. In a
separate bowl, mix together the flour, curry
powder, and baking powder. Stir in the
milk, mixing well. Add the eggs and blend.
Fold in the zucchini. Fry in hot melted
butter until golden brown on both sides.
Serve as is, or top with yogurt or sour cream.

Variation: add ¼ cup minced onion and 1
clove minced garlic to the batter.

Marie's Swedish Pancakes

Preparation time: 15 minutes
Makes: 4 servings

  2 eggs
  2 Tbsp oil
  2 cups milk
  1 cup whole wheat pastry flour
    Dash salt
    Cottage cheese
    Strawberry preserves
    Sour cream

Beat the eggs until they are light yellow. Beat in the oil and milk. Stir in the flour and salt; the mixture will be very thin. Pour a little at a time (just enough to cover the bottom) into a lightly buttered pan and fry, turning once. Serve in a stack, with cottage cheese and strawberry preserves. Let people fill and roll their own. Top with sour cream.

Guy's Custard (Danish Pancake)

Preparation time: 10 minutes to assemble,
      then 35 minutes to bake
Makes: 4 to 6 servings

  4 Tbsp butter
  ⅓ cup honey, warmed
  2½ cups milk
  ¾ cup whole wheat pastry flour
  5 eggs

Preheat oven to 375°. Heat a 9-inch deep pie pan or casserole dish. Melt the butter in the pan, coating it evenly. Mix together the honey, milk, and flour. Beat the eggs together until light golden and fluffy and stir into the honey-flour mixture until well blended. Pour into the pan and bake for 35—40 minutes. Serve immediately with preserves, syrup, or fresh fruit. This dish makes a spectacular brunch!

Peanut Gingerbread Waffles

Preparation time: 15 minutes to assemble, plus 6—8 minutes each to bake
Makes: 2 to 3 servings

    2 Tbsp vegetable oil
    ⅓ cup molasses
    2 eggs, separated
    3 Tbsp peanut butter
    1 tsp ground ginger
    ½ tsp cinnamon
    ¾ cup yogurt
    ½ cup whole wheat pastry flour
 1½ tsp baking powder
    ½ tsp salt
    1 cup wheat germ
    1 cup applesauce
    ½ cup whipping cream
    ¼ tsp vanilla extract
    ¼ tsp honey

Stir together the oil, molasses, egg yolks, peanut butter, ginger, and cinnamon until smooth and well blended. Beat in the yogurt. In a separate bowl, sift the flour with baking powder and salt. Stir flour mixture into peanut butter/molasses mixture until well blended, then stir in the wheat germ. With an eggbeater or electric mixer, whip egg whites until soft peaks form. Gently fold egg whites into batter. Bake for 6—8 minutes each, following directions for your waffle iron. Meanwhile, warm the applesauce slowly in a saucepan. Whip the cream with the vanilla and honey until soft peaks form. Serve the waffles very hot with applesauce and whipped cream.

Cottage Cheese Pancakes

Preparation time: 15 minutes
Makes: 2 servings

    3 eggs
    3 Tbsp whole wheat flour
      Dash salt
    ¾ cup cottage cheese
    3 Tbsp cream or half-and-half

Separate the eggs and beat the whites until stiff. Put the yolks, flour, salt, cottage cheese, and cream in a large bowl and combine well. Fold in the egg whites. Cook in an oiled frying pan or on a griddle. Serve with butter, preserves, or fresh fruit.

Belgian Waffles

Preparation time: 15 minutes to assemble, then 5 minutes each to bake
Makes: 6 waffles

 8 eggs, separated
 1 tsp vanilla extract
 6 Tbsp butter, melted
 1 tsp baking powder
 2 cups whole wheat pastry flour
 ½ tsp salt
 2 cups milk

Beat the egg yolks until very light. Add the vanilla and butter. In a separate bowl, stir together the baking powder, flour, and salt. Add, with the milk, to the egg mixture. Beat until smooth. Beat the egg whites until stiff and fold into the batter. Bake until golden brown (about 5 minutes), following directions for your waffle iron. Serve topped with fresh fruit or syrup.

Variation: Sprinkle the top of each waffle with chopped pecans, walnuts, or cashews before baking.

Crêpe Batter

Special requirement: a blender
Preparation time: 10 minutes to prepare batter, then 45—50 minutes to cook
Makes: about 30 crêpes

 6 eggs
 3 cups milk
 3 cups whole wheat pastry flour
 4 Tbsp butter, melted

Beat the eggs in a blender for almost a minute. Add the milk and beat several seconds. Next add the flour and melted butter a little at a time, mixing after each addition. Beat until smooth. For more perfect crêpes, let the batter stand at room temperature for 1 hour before cooking. Cook according to the instructions for your particular crêpe pan. This recipe is good for dinner, dessert, or breakfast crêpes.

This recipe can be cut in half and will still produce excellent results. The prepared crêpes can be frozen with a layer of waxed paper between each. Defrost before cooking.

Peach Brandy Crêpes

Ahead of time: prepare 30 crêpes
    (page 198)
Preparation time: overnight for marinating
    peaches, then 35 minutes to prepare
    filling
Makes: filling for 30 crêpes

    2 lbs peaches, fresh or canned
    ½ cup brandy
    ½ tsp cinnamon
    ⅛ tsp nutmeg
    ⅛ tsp ginger
    3 cups ricotta cheese
    1 cup sour cream
    ¼ cup honey
    2 tsp vanilla extract

If using canned peaches, drain well. Thinly slice the peaches, mix with the brandy and spices, and marinate in the refrigerator overnight. Mix together the ricotta, sour cream, honey, and vanilla. Blend until very smooth. Fill each crêpe with a couple of spoonfuls and roll them. Arrange the crêpes on a large ovenproof serving platter or in a shallow casserole dish. Dot the ends of each crêpe with butter and cover the pan with tinfoil. Heat in a 250° oven for 20 minutes. Sprinkle cinnamon on top. Spoon the marinated peaches over top and enjoy.

Oatmeal Porridge with Apple

Preparation time: 20 minutes
Makes: 2—4 servings

    1 cup rolled oats
    2½ cups cold water
        Salt
    1 large apple, cored and grated
    ¼ cup raisins
    ½ tsp cinnamon (optional)
        Pure maple syrup

Put the rolled oats in a saucepan with cold water and a pinch of salt. Cover and cook over medium heat for 15 minutes. Remove from heat; stir in the apple, raisins, and cinnamon. Cover and let stand for 5 minutes, or longer if you like a very thick porridge. Serve with maple syrup, and cream, milk, or yogurt if you wish.

Blackberry Crêpes

Ahead of time: prepare 30 crêpes (page 198)

Preparation time: 20 minutes to prepare topping, plus 25 minutes to prepare filling

Makes: filling for 30 crêpes

Topping:

4 cups berries
1½ cups honey

Filling:

3 cups ricotta cheese
1 cup sour cream
¼ cup honey
2 tsp vanilla extract
½ cup finely chopped walnuts

You may use commercial blackberry preserves for the topping, or prepare your own: boil the berries over medium-high heat for 10 minutes. When the juice is cooked down, add the honey and stir well to dissolve. Return to a rapid boil, then cook for 10 minutes. Drop a bit of the mixture onto a cold saucer to check for the gel. If no liquid separates, it's ready. If it is not yet gelled, cook for several minutes longer. Spoon into a serving dish and allow to cool for 20 minutes or longer.

Preheat oven to 250°. To make the filling, cream together the ricotta cheese, 1 cup sour cream, honey, and vanilla. When smooth and well blended, stir in the nuts. Place a couple of spoonsful in the center of each crêpe. Roll them and arrange on a large ovenproof serving platter. Dot the ends of each crêpe with butter and cover the platter with tinfoil. Heat in oven for about 20 minutes and serve immediately. Spoon blackberry preserves and sour cream over top, if you wish.

12

HOLIDAY DELIGHTS

Although the main purpose of this book is to bring you menus for quickly prepared repasts, we couldn't resist including some of our favorite festive treats that require more time to prepare.

November and December are the traditional times to celebrate with friends, around tables adorned with colorful and delicious foods and beverages. We hope the following recipes will become part of your holiday feasts.

Fruitcake

Special requirement: 1 five-pound angel-food cake pan **or** 5 one-pound loaf pans

Ahead of time: soften butter to room temperature

Preparation: 1½ hours to assemble, then 2½ hours to bake

Makes: one 5-pound cake or any variation thereof

This is one of those recipes that gets everything, including the kitchen sink, dirty. But the results are well worth the effort. You will need 2 very large bowls and 1 medium large bowl. The baking pans should be lined with 3 to 4 layers of waxed paper, cut to fit the bottom and sides as exactly as possible. This will ensure an even, slow baking without any burnt spots. This fruitcake does not rely on candied fruit for its flavor: it tastes more like a turn-of-the century English Christmas cake than a purchased fruitcake.

½ lb dark raisins
½ lb light raisins
1 lb pitted dates, chopped
½ lb candied fruit
½ lb dried currants
2 cups chopped walnuts
¼ cup molasses
¼ cup red wine
1 cup butter, softened
¾ cup honey
5 large eggs
2 cups sifted whole wheat pastry flour
¼ tsp salt
1 tsp cinnamon
½ tsp nutmeg
2 tsp crushed coriander seeds

Preheat oven to 275°. In one of the very large bowls, mix together the raisins, dates, candied fruit, currants, and walnuts. Pour the molasses and wine over the fruit/nut combination and toss well to coat, using two wooden spoons. Set this bowl aside.

In the other very large bowl, beat together the butter and honey until light in color. Add the eggs, one at a time. Beat well after each addition. Set aside.

In the medium bowl, sift together the flour, salt, cinnamon, and nutmeg. Place the coriander seeds between two sheets of waxed paper and crush with a rolling pin. Add the crushed seeds to the flour mixture.

Alternately add the flour mixture and fruit mixture to the butter and egg mixture. Mix well after each addition. The resulting dough will be very stiff and dominated by the dried fruits. Spoon this mixture into the waxed paper-lined baking pans. Decorate the tops with walnut halves and dried fruit if desired.

Place a pan of water on the lowest rack in the oven. Place the other rack in the middle of the oven and gently slide in the fruit-cakes. If using small loaf pans (1-pound size), bake for 2 hours. If using large loaf pans or a 5-pound angel-food cake pan, bake for 2½ hours. Test to see if the cake is done by inserting a toothpick into the center—it should come out slightly moist from all the fruit, but free of cake. Allow the fruitcake to cool for 2 hours in the pans, out of any draft. Remove from the pans and cool overnight. Wrap each cake in a brandy-soaked cloth, then store tightly wrapped in tinfoil, or in a tin, in a cool place. Re-moisten the cloth with brandy each week. Bake the cakes about 2 months before the holidays.

Pastry Shell

Preparation time: 15 minutes to assemble,
      then 1 hour to chill before rolling out
Makes: one 8-, 9-, or 10-inch double crust
      pie, **or** two 8-, 9-, or 10-inch single
      crust pies, **or** 6—8 tart shells

      2 cups whole wheat pastry flour
      ⅛ tsp salt
      ⅔ cup cold butter
6—8 Tbsp ice water

Sift the flour with the salt into a medium-sized bowl. Cut in the butter with a pastry cutter until a coarse, crumbly consistency is obtained. Sprinkle in the water, 1 table-spoonful at a time. Gently toss with a fork, pushing the mixture toward the side of the bowl after each tablespoonful is added. Repeat until all the flour mixture is moistened and the dough begins to cling together. Divide dough in half and form into two balls. Refrigerate for one hour, then roll out with a floured rolling pin on a lightly floured surface (the flour prevents the dough from sticking). Roll from the center to the edge, rotating the direction of the rolling pin until you have a ⅛-inch thick crust. Fit into a pie plate and trim the edges, leaving a little excess all around. Flute the edge by pressing dough with forefinger

against a wedge made by the forefinger and thumb of the other hand. If you're making a double-crust pie, fill the shell, then top with the other ⅛-inch thick circle of dough. Trim, then flute together with bottom crust to seal edges. Check the pie filling recipe for exact instructions. If baking unfilled, prick the bottom and bake in a preheated 450° oven for 10 minutes. This shell can be used for savory pies—such as vegetable pies and quiches—as well as for sweet pies.

Pie crust can be frozen at the ball stage, then defrosted and rolled out as needed.

Date Sugar Crust

Special Requirements: one 9-inch
    springform cake pan
Preparation time: 10 minutes
Makes: one 9-inch crust

    1½ cups date sugar
    1 cup whole wheat pastry flour
    ½ tsp salt
    1 tsp cinnamon
    ½ cup cold butter

Stir together in a bowl the date sugar, flour, salt, and cinnamon. Cut in the butter with a pastry cutter until fine and crumbly. Press into a 9-inch springform cake pan. Fill and bake according to specific recipe instructions. An excellent choice for cheesecake crust.

Graham Cracker Crust

Special Requirements: one 9-inch
    springform pan **or** 9-inch pie pan
Preparation time: 5 minutes to assemble,
    then 6 minutes to bake
Makes: one 9-inch pie crust

    1 cup graham cracker crumbs
    3 Tbsp melted butter

Preheat oven to 350°. Combine the graham cracker crumbs with the butter. Press into the bottom of a 9-inch springform cake pan (for cheesecake) or pie pan. Bake for about 6 minutes.

Pumpkin Pie

Preparation time: 15 minutes to assemble,
     then 45 minutes to bake
Makes: two 9-inch pies

- 1¾ cups pumpkin purée
- ½ tsp salt
- 1¾ cups milk
- 3 eggs, beaten
- ½ cup honey
- ⅓ cup molasses
- 2 tsp cinnamon
- ½ tsp ginger
- ½ tsp nutmeg
- ¼ tsp cloves
- 2 pie shells (see page 206)
- Whipped cream (optional)

Preheat oven to 400°. Line two 9-inch pie pans with the pastry crusts. Combine the pumpkin purée, salt, milk, eggs, honey, molasses, and spices and whisk together until well blended. Pour into the unbaked shells and bake for 15 minutes, then reduce heat to 350° and bake 30 minutes longer. Insert a knife blade into the center; if it comes out clean, the pie is done. Serve as is or with whipped cream.

Tofu Cheesecake

Special requirements: a blender and
     one 9-inch springform pan
Preparation time: 15 minutes, then
     1 hour to bake
Makes: 1 cheesecake

- 18 oz firm tofu
- 2 eggs
- ¼ cup honey, warmed
- 3 Tbsp lemon juice
- 1 tsp grated lemon peel
- 1 tsp vanilla extract
- 2 medium bananas, ripe
- 1 cup crushed pineapple, well drained
- Graham cracker crust (page 207)

Preheat oven to 325°. Drain the tofu and pat dry with paper towels. In a blender, combine the eggs, honey, lemon juice and peel, and vanilla. Blend together for several seconds. Break the tofu and bananas into chunks and add half to the blender, blending until smooth. Add remaining tofu and bananas and blend until very smooth. Pour the mixture into a bowl and stir in the crushed pineapple until well combined. Gently pour into a cooled graham cracker crust. Bake for 1 hour. Cool on a rack; chill before serving.

Cheesecake

Ahead of time: soften cream cheese to
     room temperature
Special requirement: a blender, and a
     9-inch springform pan
Preparation time: 20 minutes, then 1 hour
     to bake
Makes: one 9-inch cheesecake

- ½ cup honey
- 1½ lb cream cheese, softened
- 2 tsp lemon juice
- 2 tsp lemon rind, grated
- 2 tsp vanilla extract
- ⅛ tsp salt
- 4 eggs
- 1 Tbsp whole wheat pastry flour
- 1 cup whipping cream, very cold

Preheat oven to 350°. Put a small bowl and
your eggbeater into the freezer to chill—
you'll use them to whip the cream. Cream
together the honey and cream cheese.
Blend in the lemon juice and rind, vanilla,
and salt. In a blender, combine the eggs
and flour until smooth. Pour this into the
cream cheese mixture and stir well. Whip
the cream in the cold bowl with the cold
beater until soft peaks form. Fold this into
the cheese mixture until well combined (the
mixture will be runny). Pour into crust and
bake for 1 hour. Turn off the oven, open the
door, and leave cheesecake in the oven for
another hour. Remove from pan when
completely cooled. Eat immediately! (Or
refrigerate before serving.)

Cranberry Sauce

Preparation time: 20 minutes
Makes: 12 servings

- 1 cup water
- ½ cup honey
- 3 cups fresh cranberries

Combine the water and honey in a deep
saucepan. Bring to a boil over medium-high
heat, stirring to dissolve the honey. Add the
cranberries and continue to boil for 5—7
minutes, stirring occasionally. The skins of
the cranberries will pop as they heat, and
the sauce will boil up as it cooks. To test for
the gel point, spoon a small amount of the
hot liquid into a cold saucer. If no liquid
separates, the mixture has gelled. If it has
not yet gelled, continue to cook and stir for
several more minutes. When ready, spoon
into a serving dish or jam jar. Serve hot, or
refrigerate for several hours and serve cold.

Candied Yams in Orange Sauce

Preparation time: 50 minutes to assemble,
    then 45 minutes to bake
Makes: 6 servings

    3 large yams
    3 Tbsp butter, melted
    ½ cup fresh orange juice
       Grated peel of ½ orange
    1 tsp arrowroot powder
    ½ cup honey
    ¼ tsp nutmeg

Wash the yams and cut into large cubes. Steam until tender, about 30 minutes. Preheat oven to 350°. Allow the yams to cool several minutes, then peel off the skins and slice into ⅛-inch slices; arrange in a buttered 13 x 9-inch baking pan or 3-quart casserole dish. Mix together the butter, orange juice and peel, arrowroot, honey, and nutmeg in a saucepan. Whisk together until smooth. Bring to a boil and cook until thickened. Pour over the yams and bake, covered, for 45 minutes. These are the best-tasting yams ever!

Oyster Stuffing

Preparation time: 25 minutes to assemble,
    then 30 minutes to bake
Makes: 6-8 servings

    4 oz butter
    1 onion, chopped
    1 clove garlic, minced
    2 stalks celery, finely chopped
    ½ bell pepper, finely chopped
    1 pint oysters, chopped,
       or 2 tins smoked oysters, chopped
    ½ tsp **each** sage, rosemary, and thyme
    ½ cup parsley
    1 package (7 oz) dry bread crumbs
    4 eggs, slightly beaten
    ¾ cup broth

Preheat oven to 300°. Melt the butter in a large skillet, and sauté the onion, garlic, celery, and bell pepper until tender. Stir in the oysters and herbs. Put the bread crumbs in a large bowl and stir in the oyster mixture, eggs, and broth. Season with salt and pepper. Toss until well combined. Transfer to a well-buttered baking dish and bake, uncovered, for 30 minutes.

Stuffed Grape Leaves (Dolmas)

Ahead of time: precook brown rice to
    make 4 cups cooked
Preparation time: 90 minutes to assemble,
    then 30 minutes to bake
Makes: 6 main-course servings, or
    appetizers for 18

  1 medium eggplant
 ⅓ cup olive oil
  1 medium onion, chopped
  2 Tbsp lemon juice
1½ tsp dill weed
1½ tsp oregano
  3 cloves garlic, minced
1½ cups hot water
  1 tsp salt
    Black pepper
  4 cups brown rice, cooked

  1 jar grape leaves
  1 lb peeled tomatoes
  1 tsp basil
    Salt
    Pepper

Peel and chop the eggplant into small cubes. Heat the olive oil over medium-low heat in a large skillet and add to it the onion, eggplant, lemon juice, dill, oregano, and garlic. Stir until oil evenly coats the veg-etables. Add 1½ cups hot water and season to taste with salt and black pepper. Allow the mixture to simmer over low heat for an hour, until the eggplant is tender and the liquid is nearly evaporated. (More water can be added, if necessary, during the cooking time.) Rinse the grape leaves carefully and place them in a colander to drain.

When the eggplant mixture is thick and very soft, turn off the heat and stir in the rice. Preheat oven to 350°. Place a spoonful of the eggplant/rice mixture in each grape leaf and wrap the leaf around the filling, folding in the sides as you roll. As you stuff the leaves, arrange them on an oiled baking sheet. Place the tomatoes in a cast-iron skillet with the basil and salt and pepper to taste. Mash or chop the tomatoes into a thick sauce while cooking them over medium heat—this procedure takes about 5—10 minutes. Pour the tomato sauce over the stuffed grape leaves, cover, and bake for 30 minutes.

These are wonderful as an appetizer, or as a main course accompanied by a large salad and wine.

13

BEVERAGES

When it's cold outside, heated beverages warm and pamper us; and in warm weather, an iced beverage means instant refreshment. Beverages are a way to welcome friends to our homes, be they casual drop-ins or guests invited to share a special evening.

We've included some party-size recipes in this section as well as some you can make for just one or two.

SPECIFIC POINTERS

▶ For a fruit punch, float frozen orange slices in individual glasses instead of ice—a charming touch.

▶ In a punch bowl, block ice is much preferable to ice cubes, which tend to melt quickly, diluting your creation. Use a mold or even an empty milk carton to freeze your own block, from water or from fruit juice where appropriate.

▶ Use fresh fruit juices when available. If using frozen concentrates, dilute with only half as much water as called for on the label.

▶ All ingredients for cold beverages should be well chilled before blending.

▶ Serve hot drinks very hot, not lukewarm.

▶ When gauging how much of a beverage to make for a gathering, figure on about two 5-ounce servings per guest.

Lynn's Egg Nog

Preparation time: 15 minutes
Makes: about ½ gallon (about sixteen
    4-ounce servings)

  ¼ cup honey
  6 eggs
  ½ pt whipping cream, very cold
1½ tsp vanilla extract or
    ½ tsp almond extract
  ½ tsp ground nutmeg
  1 qt milk
    Brandy or rum (optional)

If the honey has crystallized, heat it in a small saucepan over low heat until liquid (do not boil). Allow to cool. Meanwhile, set out a large bowl and two medium bowls on your work surface. Crack the eggs and separate the whites into one of the smaller bowls. Put the yolks in the large bowl. Pour the chilled whipping cream into the third bowl. With an electric mixer or an egg-beater, beat the egg whites until foamy and thickened but not at all stiff. Now beat the cream until just beginning to thicken. Beat the yolks briefly, then add the honey and vanilla to them, beating until perfectly smooth and well blended. Now pour in the thickened cream, then the beaten egg whites, beating well after each addition.

Finally, add the nutmeg and milk and beat again until well combined. Serve cold, with a little nutmeg sprinkled on top. Serve small portions of this rich treat. You may offer brandy or rum so your guests can spike their egg nog if they wish. Cheers!

Hot Chocolate

Preparation time: 5 minutes
Makes: 1 serving

  1 cup milk
  1 Tbsp honey
  1 tsp Dutch-process ground cocoa*
    Whipped cream (optional)

Put all but 1 tablespoon of the milk in a small saucepan with the honey; heat over very low heat. In a mug, combine the cocoa and remaining tablespoon of milk until smooth. Pour the steaming, hot milk into the mug and stir to blend. Top with whipped cream if you wish.

* This cocoa is unsweetened and contains no chemical additives.

215

Yogurt Smoothie

Special requirement: a blender
Preparation time: 5 minutes
Makes: 2 servings

    1 cup plain yogurt
    6 fresh strawberries or ½ banana
    ½ cup orange or apple juice
    1 tsp to 1 Tbsp brewer's yeast*
    1 tsp honey
    6 ice cubes

Measure all ingredients except ice into blender. Whir for a few seconds. Add the ice and blend until smoothie is frothy and ice has been incorporated. A healthful, refreshing breakfast or snack.

* If brewer's yeast is new to your diet, start with 1 teaspoon and work up gradually to 3 teaspoons.

Kefir Soda

Preparation time: 2 minutes

    Soda water or sparkling mineral water
    Kefir (your favorite flavor)
    Fresh fruit (optional)

For individual servings, pour equal amounts of soda water and kefir over ice into a glass, and stir well. Garnish with fresh fruit if you wish. For larger quantities, combine equal amounts of soda water and kefir in a pitcher or punch bowl and chill. Serve over ice. This beverage is very refreshing on a summer afternoon and is an energy booster.

Fruit Soda

Preparation time: 2 minutes

    Soda water or sparkling mineral water
    Fruit juice (your favorite flavor)
    Fresh fruit (optional)

For individual servings, pour equal amounts of soda water and fruit juice over ice in a glass, and stir well. Garnish with fresh fruit if you wish. For larger quantities, combine equal amounts of juice and soda water in a pitcher or punch bowl and chill. Serve over ice. Increase the proportion of juice if you like a stronger flavor.

Spiced Cider

Preparation time: 25 minutes
Makes: 1 gallon

- ½ cup honey
- 2 tsp allspice
- 2 tsp whole cloves
- 2 tsp ground cinnamon
- 6 inches cinnamon stick
- 1 gallon apple cider

Combine all ingredients in a large kettle and slowly bring to a boil. Reduce heat; cover and simmer for 20 minutes. Before serving, strain out the spices. Serve piping hot.

Tequila Sunrise Punch

Preparation time: 15 minutes
Makes: 1½ gallons (about forty 5-ounce servings)

- 1 gallon orange juice
- 2¼ cups tequila
- 1 cup Rose's lime juice
- ½ cup grenadine syrup
- 1 lime, thinly sliced

In a large pitcher or serving bowl, mix together the orange juice, tequila, lime juice, and grenadine syrup. Add plenty of ice to chill the ingredients. Float the lime slices on top and serve immediately.

Cranberry Orange Champagne

Preparation time: 10 minutes to assemble, plus 3—4 hours to chill
Makes: 2 gallons (about fifty 5-ounce servings)

- ¼ cup liquid honey
- ½ cup fresh lemon juice
- 1 cup orange juice
- 1 cup cranberry juice
- 2 limes, very thinly sliced
- 4 fifths pink champagne or cold duck
- 1 bottle (28 oz) sparkling mineral water
- 1 cup orange liqueur

In a small bowl, stir together the honey, juices, and lime slices. Refrigerate, covered, for at least a few hours so flavors can blend. Just before serving, pour this juice mixture over ice into a large punch bowl. Add all remaining ingredients and mix well. Serve immediately, in champagne or wine goblets, perhaps garnished with a twist of lemon.

Hot Mulled Wine

Preparation time: 10 minutes to assemble,
   then 2 hours to heat slowly
Makes: 1½ gallons (about forty 5-ounce
   servings)

   2 oranges
   2 lemons
   1 gallon red wine
   ½ gallon water
   2 cups honey
   4 4-inch cinnamon sticks
   2 Tbsp whole cloves
   3 whole nutmegs

Thinly slice the oranges and lemons. Heat
the wine, water, and honey in a large
saucepan over low heat, stirring until the
honey is dissolved. Add the sliced citrus
fruits and whole herbs. Continue on a low
heat for about 2 hours. The delightful spicy
fragrance of this mulled wine fills the house,
welcoming visitors to a festive holiday get-
together.

White Mulled Wine

Preparation time: 20 minutes to assemble,
   plus 1 hour for steeping
Makes: about 50 servings

   3 qts water
   1 cup honey
  10 4-inch cinnamon sticks, broken into
      pieces
   1 Tbsp freshly grated nutmeg
  1½ tsp whole cloves
   2 qts orange juice
   5 cups lemon juice
   2 fifths dry sherry
   ½ gallon Chablis

Combine water, honey, and spices in a large
kettle. Bring to a boil and boil for 10
minutes. Remove from heat and let stand,
covered, for one hour. Strain out the
spices. Add the juices, sherry, and Chablis.
Heat through but do not boil. Float orange
slices on top.

Sangria

Preparation time: 10 minutes to assemble,
    then 1 hour to chill
Makes: ½ gallon (about 10 servings)

    1 orange
    1 lemon
       or 2 limes
    1 fifth Burgundy (about 24 oz)
    2 sliced peaches
    ½ cup fresh strawberries, quartered
    3 Tbsp brandy
    1 cup sparkling water

Juice the orange and lemon (or limes), being careful not to disturb the peels. Pour the juices into a serving bowl or pitcher and add the wine. Slice the orange and lemon peels into thin strips, and add, with the fruit and brandy, to the wine mixture. Chill in the refrigerator for one hour, to blend the flavors. Add the sparkling water just before serving.

This is wonderful with any Mexican dish, and also makes a welcome summer after-noon refresher. Serve in tall glasses over ice. Fresh mint leaves are a delightful garnish.

Gin Fizz

Special requirement: a blender
Preparation time: 3 minutes
Makes: 1 serving

    1½ oz gin
     1 egg white
        Juice of ½ lemon
     1 tsp honey, warmed
     3 drops orange-flower water*
     ½ oz Orange Curaçao™
     3 oz half-and-half

Put all ingredients into the blender, with a small amount of crushed ice. Blend until frothy. Serve in a fancy glass and dust with nutmeg. You may wish to garnish with an orange slice. This recipe makes one serving, but you can easily make several more at a time by doubling or tripling the amounts.

* Orange-flower water can be found at many gourmet food shops, and herb shops, and at some health-food stores.

NOTES

14

MENU PLANNING

Menu planning is an art. It's also a science. Our examples are well balanced nutritionally as well as creating a pleasing variety of textures and colors, and a wonderful and sometimes subtle interplay of flavors.

Begin to experiment with colors, textures, and flavors in menu planning. Trust your instincts rather than the dictates of tradition. Potatoes and rice aren't the only carbohydrate choices; salads don't have to be mostly lettuce. Let your nose, eyes, and taste buds guide you, and your creative abilities will get better and better.

Exciting and delicious meals can be served every day. Even the simple touches, such as a garnish, can enliven a meal. But for invited guests, you could dazzle them with a multiple course extravaganza. Choose a central theme or a special dish as the foundation of the meal. Choices might be your personal favorites, or which fish or vegetable is in season, or what's on sale at the market. You may want to serve a tried-and-true dish, or intrigue and delight all with something new and "exotic." Often an international theme seems appropriate. Even the weather might suggest a main dish; for example, the first storm of winter almost pleads for a hearty soup or stew. Or maybe the peach tree is overloaded or a birthday cake is needed; then the dessert can guide the choices for the other courses.

A few minutes carefully planning a menu and organizing recipe requirements will help create a relaxed and enjoyable experience. Consider your own style and pace in the kitchen as well as the time allotment for the particular meal. An unfamiliar recipe generally takes a bit more time—when trying new dishes make the rest of the meal from familiar recipes. When possible, prepare part of the meal ahead of time, leaving only a few items that require your full attention for the last moment. If guests are willing and able, don't hesitate to recruit them. Not only can they toss the salad, they can pour you a glass of wine and keep you company.

The following menu plans are organized by season to inspire the use of fresh produce. We confess to being spoiled by California's long growing season. Here early autumn brings an abundance of zucchini, eggplant, and tomatoes. In your area fruits and vegetables may be available earlier or later depending upon the climate.

With good nutrition, good tastes, and good times in mind, we offer detailed suggestions for satisfying meals that are like symphonies, where every element is essential to the harmonious whole.

Spring

Though there is still a chill in the air, the sprouting of new greenery and the opening of flowers convince us that spring has arrived. The days lengthen as the vernal equinox approaches, and our appetites lessen in anticipation of warmer weather. The coarser, cool-season fruits and vegetables are still available and constitute a considerable part of our diets, but early cherries and strawberries and the season's first asparagus delight our senses with vibrant colors and sweet and delicate flavors. An occasional storm may still bombard us, but we are beginning to crave lighter repasts.

Summer

In the heat of summer, food becomes lower priority for most of us. But our increased summer activities call for special attention to nutrition. Fresh fruits and vegetables are in abundance at this time—to be enjoyed raw or with minimum preparation. The appetite ebbs as the summer solstice approaches. Our bodies crave the refreshment of crisp vegetables or fruit salads and icy beverages. Our focus shifts to the simplest dishes, sending our stoves into semi-retirement.

Autumn

After months of carefree activity in the summer sun, in autumn we spend more time at home. Those who garden are busy canning the last of summer's bounty. Our sweaters and coats come out of mothballs in anticipation of the coming chill. The gold and orange colors of falling leaves are also seen in vegetables and flowers, and the autumn sunsets. After a summer's worth of salads, we hunger for hot and hearty soups and stews. With the onset of cooler evenings, the kitchen again becomes the heart of our homes.

Winter

When it's stormy outside it's a pleasure to come home to a hot beverage and a warm and cozy kitchen. Winter is a perfect time for baking, as friends and family linger near the stove to bask in the warmth and wonderful aromas. The temptation to eat a cookie just out of the oven overpowers us and we don't mind risking burned fingers and tongues. Winter is a time to huddle together, sharing hugs and stories around a fire, and fine hearty meals.

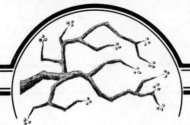

SPRING SAMPLER

Asparagus Omelette
Whole fresh strawberries
Toasted English muffins
or Whole-grain bread

· · · · · · · · · · · · · · ·

Cottage Cheese Pancakes
Orange wedges
Coffee, tea, or champagne

· · · · · · · · · · · · · · ·

Crab-Egg Dip
Garbanzo Sesame Spread
Assorted crackers
Fresh vegetable sticks
Brie or Camembert cheese
Chilled Chardonnay

· · · · · · · · · · · · · · ·

Spinach Soup with Lemon
Finger Salad with Herb Curry Dip
Sourdough rolls
Cherry Cobbler

· · · · · · · · · · · · · · ·

Fettucine Salad with Mushrooms
Hot Tarragon Steamed Artichokes
with Dill Dip
Carrot sticks
Fresh fruit and cheeses

Tofu Patties with Basic White Sauce
Steamed bulghur
Steamed broccoli
Celery Seed Cabbage Salad

· · · · · · · · · · · · · · ·

Baked Sole Amandine
Asparagus with Hollandaise Sauce
Steamed potatoes
Papaya Compote

· · · · · · · · · · · · · · ·

Poached Fish
Steamed carrots and broccoli
Rice with Parsley
Leafy green salad with
Simple Vinaigrette Dressing

· · · · · · · · · · · · · · ·

Chinese Vegetables
Fried Rice
Tahini Cookies
Jasmine or green tea

· · · · · · · · · · · · · · ·

Pasta with Cauliflower-Tomato Sauce
Leafy green salad with French Dressing
Bread sticks
Simple Fruit and Cheese Dessert

SUMMER SAMPLER

Whole Wheat Scones
Breakfast cheese
Cantaloupe slices
Hot or iced tea or coffee

. . . .

Glazed Lemon Bread
Ratatouille
Champagne

. . . .

Avocado and crab chunks
with Cocktail Sauce
Shrimp Spread
Teleme cheese
Assorted crackers
Fresh vegetable sticks

. . . .

Grilled Tofu Kabobs with Teriyaki Sauce
Potato Salad
Chilled steamed green beans with
Simple Vinaigrette Dressing
Chocolate Chip Cookies

. . . .

Pasta al Pesto
Leafy green salad with Simple
Vinaigrette Dressing
Pickled Mushrooms
Spumoni ice cream

Salmon with Caper Sauce
Tossed green salad with
Sesame Tahini Dressing
French bread
Fruit Crisp
Well-chilled white wine

. . . .

Curried Rice Pilaf
Creamy Zucchini Curry
Cucumber Stick Salad
Gingered Carrots and Broccoli
Strong mint tea, iced

. . . .

Eggplant Patties
Creamy Dill Sauce
Dill Tomatoes on lettuce bed
Bread sticks
Ricotta and Fruit Salad

. . . .

Fresh Tomato/Squash Sauté
Steamed rice or bulghur
Tarragon Tossed Salad
Steamed corn on the cob

. . . .

Peggy's Green Pea Salad
Parmesan Potatoes
Grilled fresh fish
Fruit Soda

AUTUMN SAMPLER

Soft-Boiled Eggs with Toast Fingers
Honeydew melon slices
Purple grapes
Hot tea

. . . .

Zucchini Pancakes
Sour Cream Dill Sauce
Tomato slices with parsley sprigs

. . . .

Bran Muffins
Almost Waldorf Salad
Kefir Soda

. . . .

Ratatouille
Polenta with Cheese
Leafy green salad with Buttermilk
Tahini Dressing

. . . .

Chile Relleño Casserole
Guacamole with chips
Steamed summer squash
Beer

. . . .

Zucchini Chowder
Cornbread
Cole Slaw

Sweet & Sour Vegetables and Tofu
Soba
Green Beans with Sunflower Seeds

. . . .

Stuffed Manicotti
Bread sticks
Leafy green salad with Simple
Vinaigrette Dressing
Hearty red wine

. . . .

Shrimp Creole
Steamed rice
Steamed broccoli
Tossed green salad with French Dressing

. . . .

Eggplant and Fresh Basil Soup
Cheese-topped Bread
Fresh vegetable sticks
Applesauce Cake

. . . .

Sesame Tofu
Lemony Apples and Carrots
Bulghur Millet Pilaf
Butterscotch Brownies

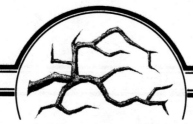

WINTER SAMPLER

Poached eggs on toast with avocado slices
Quick Rarebit Sauce
Tomato slices
Hot tea
· · · · · · · · · · · · · · · · · · ·
Belgian Waffles
Orange slices
Hot coffee or tea
· · · · · · · · · · · · · · · · · · ·
Cheese Soup
Bread sticks
Mixed vegetable salad
with Avocado Dressing
Spice Cake
· · · · · · · · · · · · · · · · · · ·
Potato Soup
Cheese Dill Muffins
Tossed green salad with
your favorite dressing
Red wine
· · · · · · · · · · · · · · · · · · ·
Carrot Curry Soup
Vegetable Curry
Bulghur Millet Pilaf
Plain yogurt
Curry Condiments
· · · · · · · · · · · · · · · · · · ·
Fettucine al Burro
Steamed brussels sprouts and carrots
Bread sticks
Finger salad with oil and vinegar
White wine

Salmon Log
Unsalted rye crackers
Mushrooms Paprika
Biscuits
Steamed broccoli
· · · · · · · · · · · · · · · · · · ·
Stuffed Artichokes
Steamed rice
Tossed green salad with
Mustard Sesame Dressing
Applesauce Cake
· · · · · · · · · · · · · · · · · · ·
Stove-Top Fish
Parsley Rice
Brussels Sprouts with Sour Cream
English Baked Custard
Thumbprint Cookies
· · · · · · · · · · · · · · · · · · ·
Red Snapper with Mushroom Topping
Steamed Rice
Sunshine Cauliflower
Dry white wine
· · · · · · · · · · · · · · · · · · ·
Tofu Tacos
Spicy Citrus Salad
Spanish Rice
Sangria
· · · · · · · · · · · · · · · · · · ·
Bay shrimp on lettuce leaves
with Cocktail Sauce
Cheese Fondue
Chocolate Swirl Cake

227

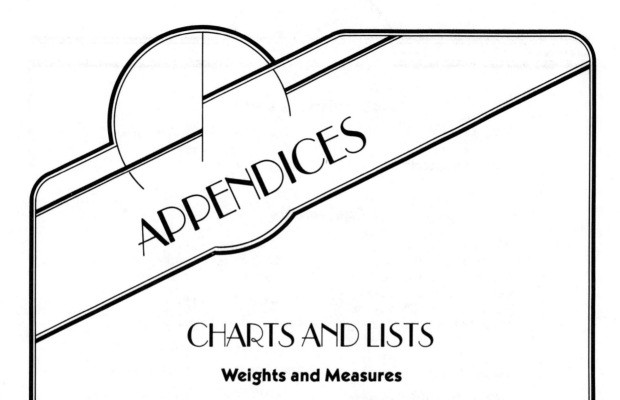

APPENDICES

CHARTS AND LISTS

Weights and Measures

The following chart lists dry measurements first and provides the equivalent liquid measure in parentheses. Liquids should be measured in a glass measuring cup placed on a flat surface, filled to the desired amount, and read at eye level. Dry ingredients should be piled lightly with a spoon or scoop into a measuring cup. Don't shake the cup to settle the contents unless specified in the recipe you are following. If you use fractional individual measuring cups (usually available in a set of four sizes), you can level off the contents with a straightedge, such as the handle of a wooden spoon, to insure accurate measurement. Measuring spoons should also be leveled for accuracy. Some recipes call for a heaping teaspoon; this means all that the spoon can hold without leveling off. To measure liquids, just fill the appropriate spoon to the top.

Abbreviations Used

oz = ounce(s)
lb = pound(s)
tsp = teaspoon(s)

Tbsp = tablespoon(s)
pt, pts = pint(s)
qt, qts = quart(s)

Equivalents

A pinch or dash = less than ⅛ tsp
1 Tbsp = 3 tsp (½ fluid oz)
⅛ cup = 2 Tbsp (1 fluid oz)
¼ cup = 4 Tbsp (2 fluid oz)
⅓ cup = 5⅓ Tbsp (2⅔ fluid oz)
½ cup = 8 Tbsp (4 fluid oz) (1 gill)
⅔ cup = 10⅔ Tbsp (5⅓ fluid oz)
¾ cup = 12 Tbsp (6 fluid oz)
1 cup = 16 Tbsp (8 fluid oz)

2 cups = 1 pint (16 fluid oz)
2 pints = 1 quart
4 quarts = 1 gallon
8 quarts = 1 peck
4 pecks = 1 bushel
(bushel weight varies with type of fruit)

1 gram = 0.035 oz
1 oz = 28.35 grams
16 oz = 1 lb
1 kilogram = 2.21 lb
1 lb = 453.59 grams
2 cups butter = 1 lb
1 lb cheese = 4 cups grated

5 large eggs = 1 cup
8 egg whites = 1 cup
16 egg yolks = 1 cup

4 cups flour = 1 lb

1 cup uncooked macaroni 2 cups cooked

1 cup uncooked noodles 1¼ cups cooked

1 cup uncooked rice 2 cups cooked

1½ lb apples = 1 qt sliced
3 cups dried apricots = 1 lb

3 large bananas = 1 lb
2 cups dates = 1 lb
1 large lemon = about ¼ cup juice
1 medium orange = about ½ cup juice

2½ cups prunes = 1 lb
2½ cups raisins = 1 lb

1 cup nutmeats = 5 oz

1 lb potatoes = 4 medium-size potatoes
1 lb tomatoes = 3 medium-size tomatoes

Metric Conversion Table

To change	to	Multiply by
ounces (oz)	grams (g)	28
pounds (lbs)	kilograms (kg)	0.45
teaspoons (tsp)	milliliters (ml)	5
tablespoons (Tbsp)	milliliters (ml)	15
fluid ounces (oz)	milliliters (ml)	30
cups	liters (l)	0.24
pints (pts)	liters (l)	0.47
quarts (quarts)	liters (l)	0.95
gallons	liters (l)	3.8
degrees Fahrenheit	degrees Centigrade	$5/9$ after subtracting 32

Oven Temperatures

Slow 250—300°F
Moderately slow 325°F
Moderate 350°F
Moderately quick 375°F
Moderately hot 400°F
Hot 425—450°F
Very hot 475—500°F

Storage Temperatures

Fruits and vegetables 34—35°F
Dairy products 38—46°F
Frozen foods 0—20°F
Breads 0—46°F
Oils 38—46°F

TRICKS OF THE TRADE

In an attempt to make this cookbook as complete as possible, we want to present some tidbits of information that are worth their weight in caviar. Rather than scatter them throughout the book, we've brought them all together for convenient study. Here, then, are some facts you never knew you wanted to know:

▶ Before measuring honey, coat a measuring cup or spoon with a trace of oil to prevent sticking.

▶ If your honey crystallizes (as all raw honey will) set the jar in a pan of hot water over very low heat until the honey liquefies again.

▶ To prevent bananas, avocados, and other low-acid foods from darkening after they've been sliced or mashed, brush with or mix in some lemon juice.

▶ To get the most juice from a lemon, immerse it for a moment in very hot water or roll it vigorously between the palm of your hand and a hard, flat surface before cutting.

▶ When frying or sauteing, heat the oil before adding foods, to prevent excessive greasiness.

▶ To keep slices of pie from sticking to the pie plate, wrap a hot, wet towel underneath and around the plate for a few minutes before cutting.

▶ To peel garlic, crush each clove gently with the flat of a knife blade. The skin will burst loose.

▶ To absorb refrigerator odors, keep an open carton of baking soda on the top shelf.

▶ Hard-boiled eggs will peel more easily if left under cold running water for a minute or two immediately after boiling.

▶ If you want to know whether an egg in your refrigerator is raw or hard-boiled, spin it on a flat surface. If it spins evenly like a top, it's hard-boiled. If it wobbles around, it's raw.

▶ Sauces containing eggs or milk may curdle if boiled, so heat them gently.

▶ To whip cream, use chilled beaters and bowls. To whip egg whites, have tools and eggs at room temperature.

▶ Warmed bowls or plates keep food hot longer.

▶ Before peeling and cutting onions, put them in the freezer for several minutes. You'll shed fewer tears.

▶ To plump raisins, soak them in milk or juice for several minutes before using.

▶ For homemade bread crumbs, dry slightly stale bread cubes or slices in the oven, place in a paper bag, and crush with a rolling pin.

▶ Slightly stale and hardened bread or crackers can be refreshed if they are put for a few minutes in a warm oven with a pan of hot water.

▶ Water boils faster when heated in a covered kettle.

▶ To clean built-up crust off a griddle, heat it, then pour on a small amount of vinegar or pickle brine and scrape with a spatula. After build-up loosens, wipe it off with a damp sponge.

RECOMMENDED READING

Basic Nutritional Guides:

Are You Confused? by Paavo Airola, Health Plus, 1971
Consumer Beware by Beatrice Trum Hunter, Touchstone, Simon and Schuster, 1972
Let's Eat Right to Keep Fit by Adelle Davis, Formur Intl., 1970
Let's Get Well by Adelle Davis, Formur Intl., 1972
Sugar Blues by William Duffy, Warner Books, 1976

Good Cookbooks:

Book of Miso and Book of Tofu by William Shurtleff and Akiko Aoyagi, Ballantine, 1981 and 1979
Diet for a Small Planet by Frances Moore Lappe, Ballantine, 1975
International Vegetarian Cookery by Sonya Richmond, Arco, 1965
Laurel's Kitchen by Laurel Robertson, Carol Flinders, and Bronwen Godfrey, Bantam, 1978
The Natural Foods Cookbook by Beatrice Trum Hunter, Simon and Schuster, 1969
Recipes for a Small Planet by Ellen Buchman Ewald, Ballantine, 1975
Tassajara Bread Book and Tassajara Cooking Book by Ed Brown, Shambhala Publications, 1970 and 1973
The Vegetarian Epicure by Anna Thomas, Random House, Knopf, 1972
The Vegetarian Epicure, Book Two by Anna Thomas, Random House, Knopf, 1978
Vegetarian Gourmet Cookery by Alan Hooker, 101 Productions, 1970
World-of-the-East Vegetarian Cooking by Madhur Jaffrey, Alfred A. Knopf, 1981

Canning and Food Preservation:

Putting It Up With Honey by Susan Geiskopf, Quicksilver Productions, 1979

GLOSSARY

Al dente—Literally means "to the tooth." Describes vegetables or pasta cooked until slightly tender but not soft.

Bake—To cook, covered or uncovered, in an oven.

Baste—To moisten foods during cooking, using pan drippings or a special sauce, to add flavor and prevent drying.

Beat—To make a mixture smooth by incorporating air with a brisk whipping or stirring motion, using a spoon or electric mixer.

Blanch—To immerse (usually for a minute) in boiling water or steam, to loosen skin for easier peeling.

Blend—To combine two or more ingredients thoroughly until the mixture is smooth and uniform.

Boil—To cook in liquid that has been heated to the boiling point (where bubbles rise to the surface and break), or to heat a liquid mixture to that point. A full rolling boil is when bubbles form rapidly throughout the mixture.

Braise—To cook slowly, with a small amount of liquid, in a tightly covered pan—on top of the range or in the oven.

Bread—To coat with crumbs or batter before cooking.

Broil—To cook by direct heat, usually in a broiler or over coals.

Candy—To cook in sugar or syrup, as with sweet potatoes or carrots. For fruit or fruit peel, to cook in heavy syrup until translucent and well coated.

Chill—To reduce temperature by placing in the refrigerator.

Chop—To cut food into pieces about the size of peas.

Cool—To remove from heat source and let stand at room temperature.

Cream—To beat with spoon or electric mixer until mixture is soft and smooth. When referring to combining butter and sugar, to beat until light and fluffy.

Cut in—To mix butter with dry ingredients using a pastry cutter, a fork, or two knives.

Dice—To cut food into small cubes of uniform size and shape.

Dissolve—To disperse a dry substance in a liquid.

Dredge—To sprinkle or coat with flour.

Flake—To break lightly, usually with a fork, into small shreds.

Fold—To add ingredients gently to a mixture. Using a spatula, cut down through mixture, go across bottom and up and over, close to the surface. Turn bowl frequently for even distribution.

French cut—To cut on a slant, as with string beans or carrots.

Fry—To cook in hot oil.

Glaze—A mixture which hardens or becomes firm when applied to food, adding flavor and a glossy appearance. Also, to coat with such a mixture.

Grate—To rub on a grater, separating the food into very fine particles.

Hard-boil—For eggs, to place in a large pan of cold salted water, bring to a boil, and cook for 10 minutes.

Knead—To work dough with the heel of the hand with a pressing and folding motion.

Marinate—To allow a food to stand in a prepared liquid to tenderize or to add flavor.

Mix—To combine ingredients until evenly distributed.

Pit—To remove pits from fruit.

Poach—To cook in hot liquid, being careful that food holds its shape while cooking.

Precook—To cook food, partially or completely, before final cooking or reheating.

Roux—A cooked paste of butter and flour; the first stage in making many sauces.

Sauté—To brown or cook in a small amount of hot oil or butter. First the pan is heated, then the oil is added and heated, then the food is added.

Scald—To bring to a temperature just below the boiling point; tiny bubbles form at the edge of the pan.

Scallop—To bake food, usually in a casserole dish, with sauce or liquid. Crumbs are often sprinkled on top.

Shred—To rub on a shredder to form long and very narrow pieces.

Sift—To put dry ingredients through a sieve or sifter to make mixture uniformly fine.

Simmer—To cook in liquid over low heat at a low temperature (185—210°F), so that bubbles form at a slow rate and burst before reaching the surface.

Soft peaks—To beat egg whites or whipping cream until peaks are formed when beaters are lifted out, but the tips of the peaks curl over.

Steam—To cook in steam, with or without pressure. A small amount of boiling water is used in a tightly covered pot, with the food suspended above the water on some type of rack.

Steep—To extract color, flavor, or other qualities from a substance by leaving it in liquid just below the boiling point, as when making tea.

Stew—To simmer slowly in a small amount of liquid.

Stiff peaks—To beat egg whites until peaks form that stand up straight when beaters are lifted out. They should still be moist and glossy.

Stir—To mix ingredients with a circular motion until well blended.

Toss—To mix ingredients lightly.

Whip—To beat rapidly to incorporate air and produce expansion, as with heavy cream or egg whites.

Zest—The finely grated peel of a citrus fruit.

INDEX

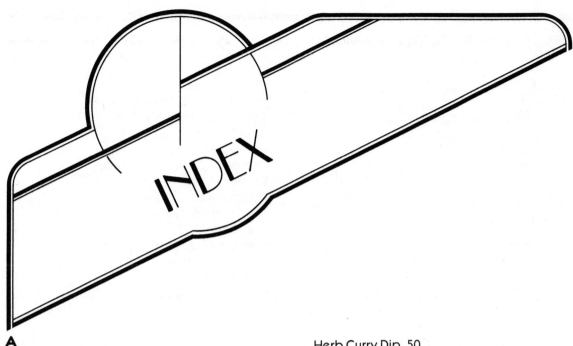

INDEX

A

Abbreviations used, 230
Acorn squash, stuffed, 127
Agar-agar, 86
Appetizers, 37—51
  All-American Deviled Eggs, 40
  Australian Clam Dip, 43
  Cheese-topped Bread, 39
  Crab Egg Dip, 44
  Crab Puffs, 45
  Crab Spread, 43
  Deviled Eggs, 39
  Garbanzo Sesame Spread, 42
  Garlic Tofu Spread, 42
  Ginger Dip, 47
  Guacamole, 48
  Herb Cheese Ball, 49

  Herb Curry Dip, 50
  Hot Crabmeat Dip, 44
  Jennifer's Popcorn, 51
  Refreshing Cream Cheese Spread, 49
  Ricotta Avocado Spread, 41
  Salmon Log, 46
  Savory Cheese Spread, 50
  Shrimp Spread, 46
  Simplest Dips, 38
  Simplest Spreads, 38
  Smoked Oyster Roll, 47
  Stuffed Mushrooms, 51
  Tofu Avocado Spread, 41
  Tofu Egg Salad, 40
Apples,
  almost Waldorf salad, 56
  banana-peanut fruit salad, 55

cobbler, 180
crisp, 179
lemony, carrots and, 104
oatmeal porridge, 199
ricotta fruit salad, 55
Applesauce
cake, 174
saucy ginger cookies, 183
Arrowroot, 86
Artichokes
steaming time, 99
stuffed, 128
tarragon steamed, with dill dip, 101
Avocado
dressing, 67
guacamole, 48
poached eggs with cheese and, 191
quesadillas, 132
ricotta spread, 41
spicy citrus salad, 56
tofu spread, 41

B

Baked Goods and Sweets, 163—185
Applesauce Cake, 174
Banana Bran Muffins, 167
Biscuits, 169
Bran Muffins, 167
Brownies, 178
Butterscotch Brownies, 178
Carob Frosting, 176
Carrot Cake, 172
Cheese Dill Muffins, 168

Cherries Jubilee, 181
Chocolate Chip Cookies, 182
Chocolate Swirl Cake, 174
Corn Muffins, 168
Cornbread (or muffins), 168
Cranberry Orange Nut Bread, 171
Cream Cheese Frosting, 177
English Baked Custard, 179
Fruit Cobbler, 180
Fruit Crisp, 179
Glazed Lemon Bread, 170
Honey Nut Bread, 169
Oat Raisin Muffins, 166
Orange Bundt Cake, 173
Papaya Compote, 182
Peaches Flambé, 181
Peanut Banana Morsels, 185
Peanut Butter Cookies, 185
Peanut-Oatmeal Cookies, 184
Peggy's Banana Nut Bread, 171
Peggy's Rice Pudding, 180
Saucy Ginger Cookies, 183
Simple Fruit and Cheese Dessert, 182
Spice Cake, 176
Strawberry Glazed Cake, 175
Tahini Cookies, 184
Thumbprint Cookies, 183
Whipped Cream, 177
Whole wheat Scones, 166
Zucchini Bread, 172
Bananas
bran muffins, 167
nut bread, 171

peanut fruit salad, 55
peanut morsels, 185
ricotta fruit salad, 55
Bean curd (see tofu)
Beets, cooked, 101
Beverages, 213—219
    Cranberry Orange Champagne, 217
    Fruit Soda, 216
    Gin Fizz, 219
    Hot Chocolate, 215
    Hot Mulled Wine, 218
    Kefir Soda, 216
    Lynn's Egg Nog, 215
    Sangria, 219
    Spiced Cider, 217
    Tequila Sunrise Punch, 217
    White Mulled Wine, 218
    Yogurt Smoothie, 216
Breads,(also see nut breads)
    about, 26, 164-165
    cheese-topped, 39
    garlic tofu spread for, 42
    glazed lemon, 170
Brewer's yeast
    popcorn, 51
    yogurt smoothie, 216
Broccoli,
    soup
      cream of, 82
      with cheese and ginger, 82
    gingered carrots and, 103
    spicy stir-fried vegetables, 125
    steaming time, 99

Broths, 73
Brussels Sprouts
    steaming time, 99
    with nutmeg, 106
    with sour cream, 102
Bulghur
    greens and grains, 121
    millet pilaf, 116
    salad, 64
Butterfish
    in cream sauce, 154
    stove-top, 156
Buttermilk
    apple nut pancakes, 195
    bran muffins, 167
    quick rarebit sauce, 92
    spice cake, 176
    tahini dressing, 65
    whole wheat scones, 166

C

Cabbage
    salad
      celery seed, 59
      spicy citrus, 56
    steaming time, 99
Cakes or coffee cakes
    about, 163-165
    applesauce, 174
    carrot, 172
    chocolate swirl, 174
    fruitcake, 204
    glazed lemon bread, 170

orange bundt, 173
spice, 176
strawberry glazed, 175
Cantaloupe
ricotta fruit salad, 55
Carob
brownies, 178
chip cookies, 182
frosting, 176
Carrots
almost Waldorf salad, 56
cake, 172
curry soup, 74
gingered, broccoli and, 103
lemony apples and, 104
steamed, 104
steaming time, 99
with tarragon, 103
Cauliflower
steaming time, 99
sunshine, 102
tomato sauce for pasta, 136
vegetable curry, 126
Cheese, (also see cream cheese, ricotta cheese,
and cottage cheese)
about, 28
asparagus omelettes, 193
au gratin potatoes, 105
ball, 49
blue cheese dressing, 66
broccoli soup, 82
chile relleño casserole, 131
chive-Parmesan noodles, 117

crab puffs, 45
enchiladas, 131
fettucine al burro, 138
fettucine Alfredo, 137
fondue, 133
muffins, 168
poached eggs with avocado, 191
poached eggs with Parmesan, 190
polenta with, 117
quesadillas, 132
quick rarebit sauce, 92
sauce, 88
soup, 77
stuffed mushrooms, 51
Cherries
cobbler, 180
jubilee, 181
Chinese 5-spice, 32
Clam
chowder, 75
dip, 43
steamed, 157
Cocktail sauce, 68
Cod
fish stew, 77
in cream sauce, 154
poached fish, 153
Cookies
about, 163-165
chocolate chip, 182
peanut banana morsels, 185
peanut butter, 185
peanut-oatmeal, 184

saucy ginger, 183
tahini, 184
thumbprint, 183
Cornmeal
  cornbread, 168
  muffins, 168
  polenta with cheese, 117
Cornstarch, 86
Cottage cheese
  herb curry dip, 50
  pancakes, 197
Crab
  egg dip, 44
  hot dip, 44
  puffs, 45
  spread, 43
Cracked wheat (see bulghur)
Cranberries
  orange nut bread, 171
  sauce, 209
Cream cheese
  cheesecake, 209
  clam dip, 43
  crab spread, 43
  crabmeat dip, 44
  frosting, 177
  herb cheese ball, 49
  salmon log, 46
  shrimp spread, 46
  smoked oyster roll, 47
  spread, 49, 50
Crêpes
  batter, 152 & 198 (same recipe)

blackberry, 200
oyster, 152
peach brandy, 199
Crusts
  date sugar, 207
  graham cracker, 207
  pastry shell, 206
Cucumbers
  sour cream, 62
  stick salad, 62
Curry
  carrot soup, 74
  herb dip, 50
  rice casserole, 115
  rice pilaf, 115
  sauce, 88
  shrimp, 158
  spinach soup, 79
  tofu and onions, 146
  vegetable, 126
  vegetable salad, 60
  yogurt dressing, 65
  zucchini, creamy, 108
Curry concoction, 31
Curry condiment plate, 126

D

Dairy products, 27-28
Desserts, (also see cookies)
  about, 163-165
  applesauce cake, 174
  baked custard, 179
  banana-nut bread, 171

butterscotch brownies, 178
brownies, 178
carrot cake, 172
cheesecake, 209
cherries jubilee, 181
chocolate swirl cake, 174
cranberry orange nut bread, 171
fruit cobbler, 180
fruit crisp, 179
fruitcake, 204
glazed lemon bread, 170
honey nut bread, 169
orange bundt cake, 173
papaya compote, 182
peaches flambé, 181
pumpkin pie, 208
rice pudding, 180
simple fruit and cheese, 182
spice cake, 176
strawberry glazed cake, 175
tofu cheesecake, 208
zucchini bread, 172
Dips
    clam, 43
    crab egg, 44
    garbanzo sesame spread, 42
    ginger, 47
    guacamole, 48
    herb curry, 50
    hot crabmeat, 44
    ricotta avocado spread, 41
    salsa, 94

simplest, 38
tofu egg salad, 40

E

Eggplant
    patties, 129
    sesame, 129
    soup with fresh basil, 74
    sweet and sour vegetables and tofu, 148
    ratatouille, 127
Eggs
    about, 28, 187-188
    all-American deviled, 40
    asparagus and cheese omelette, 193
    baked, 192
    cooking techniques
        boiled, hard or soft, 188
        fried, 188
        omelette, 189
        poached, 188
        scrambled, 189
    crab dip, 44
    custard, 179
    deviled, 39
    egg nog, 215
    hard-boiled, 188
    marinated sauce, for pasta, 138
    poached, 188
        "Benedict" style, 191
        with cheese and avocado, 191
        with Parmesan cheese, 190
    rice pudding, 180

scrambled, and onions, 192
soft-boiled, 188, 190
tofu salad, 40

F

Fish,(also see names of fish)
  about, 150-151
  cooking methods, 151
  Fish and Seafood Main Courses,, 150—161
    Baked Fish with Cream Sauce, 154
    Baked Sole Almandine, 154
    Oyster Crêpes, 159
    Poached Fish, 153
    Quick & Simple Scampi, 159
    Red Snapper with Mushroom Topping, 155
    Salmon with Caper Sauce, 153
    Shrimp Creole, 157
    Shrimp Curry, Traditional Style, 158
    Shrimp Oyster Bake, 160
    Sole Fillets with Capers, 159
    Steamed Clams, 157
    Stove-top Fish, 156
    Stuffed Fish, 156
  stew, 77
Flour, 26
Frosting
  carob, 176
  cream cheese, 177
  orange glaze topping, 173
  strawberry glaze, 175
  whipped cream, 177
Fruits,(also see names of fruits)
  and cheese dessert, 182

cobbler, 180
crisp, 179
fruitcake, 204
salad
  banana-peanut, 55
  ricotta, 55

G

Glazes
  lemon, 170
  orange, 173
  strawberry, 175
Glossary, 235
Goat's milk, 27
Gomasio, 32
Grains (also see rice, oats, cornmeal, millet)
  about, 25
  Grain and Pasta Accompaniments, 111—117
    Bulghur-Millet Pilaf, 116
    Chive-Parmesan Noodles, 117
    Curried Rice Pilaf, 115
    Curry-Rice Casserole, 115
    Fried Rice, 114
    Polenta with Cheese, 117
    Poppy Seed Noodles, 116
    Rice with Parsley, 113
    Saffron Rice, 113
    Spanish Rice, 114

H

Herbs
  about, 30-31, 98
  Chinese 5-spice, 32

curry concoction, 31
gomasio, 32
herb blends, 31-32
herb companions for vegetables, 98
Italian seasoning, 31
pumpkin pie blend, 32
Holiday Delights, 203—211
Candied Yams in Orange Sauce, 210
Cheesecake, 209
Cranberry Sauce, 209
Date Sugar Crust, 207
Dolmas, 211
Fruitcake, 204
Graham Cracker Crust, 207
Oyster Stuffing, 210
Pastry Shell, 206
Pumpkin Pie, 208
Stuffed Grape Leaves, 211
Tofu Cheesecake, 208
Hydrogenation, 30

I

Icing (see frosting)
Italian seasoning, 31

L

Leeks, potato soup, 79

M

Macaroni (see pasta)
Marmite", 73
Menu planning, 221-227

Metric conversion table, 231
Millet
bulghur pilaf, 116
greens and grains, 121
Miso, 33, 73
Morning Meals,, 187—201
Apple Nut Pancakes, 195
Asparagus and Cheese Omelette, 193
Baked Eggs, 192
Belgian Waffles, 198
Blackberry Crêpes, 200
Cottage Cheese Pancakes, 197
Crêpe Batter, 198
Danish Pancake, 196
Guy's Custard (Danish Pancake), 196
Hash Browned Potatoes, 194
Marie's Swedish Pancakes, 196
Oatmeal Porridge with Apple, 199
Orange Whole Wheat Pancakes, 194
Peach Brandy Crêpes, 199
Peanut Gingerbread Waffles, 197
Poached Eggs, "Benedict" Style, 191
Poached Eggs with Cheese and Avocado, 191
Poached Eggs with Parmesan Cheese, 190
Scrambled Eggs with Onions, 192
Soft-boiled Eggs with Toast Fingers, 190
Zucchini Pancakes, 195
Muffins
about, 163-165
banana bran, 167
bran, 167
cheese dill, 168

corn, 168
oat raisin, 166
Mushrooms
    creamy tofu and, 149
    fettucine Alfredo, 137
    fettucine salad with, 59
    paprika, 123
    pickled, 65
    shrimp oyster bake, 160
    stove-top fish, 156
    stroganoff, 122
    stuffed, 51
    stuffed artichokes, 128
    tacos, 130
    tostadas, 130
    wine sauce, 89

N

Nut breads
    about, 163-165
    banana, 171
    cranberry orange, 171
    honey nut, 169
    zucchini, 172
Nuts, 29

O

Oats
    porridge with apple, 199
    raisin muffins, 166
Oils, 30

Oranges
    banana peanut fruit salad, 55
    bundt cake, 173
    candied yams, 210
    cranberry nut bread, 171
    spicy citrus salad, 56
    whole wheat pancakes, 194
Oven temperatures, 231
Oyster
    crêpes, 152
    roll, 47
    shrimp bake, 160
    stuffing, 210

P

Pancakes
    about, 187-188
    apple nut, 195
    cottage cheese, 197
    crêpes, 152, 198
    Danish, 196
    Swedish, 196
    whole wheat, orange, 194
    zucchini, 195
Pasta
    about, 27, 134
    chive-Parmesan noodles, 117
    grain and pasta accompaniments, 111
    Pasta Main Courses,, 134—141
        Fettucine Alfredo with Onions and
            Mushrooms, 137
        Fettucine al Burro, 138
        Lasagna, 141

Pasta al Pesto, 139
Pasta with Cauliflower-Tomato Sauce, 136
Pasta with Marinated Egg Sauce, 138
Soba with Fried Vegetables, 135
Stuffed Manicotti, 140
poppy seed noodles, 116
salads
    fettucine, with mushrooms, 59
    macaroni, 58
    shrimp and macaroni, 58
with cauliflower-tomato sauce, 136
with marinated egg sauce, 138
Pastry shell, 206
Peaches
    brandy crêpes, 199
    cobbler, 180
    crisp, 179
    flambé, 181
Peanut butter
    banana morsels, 185
    cookies, 185
    gingerbread waffles, 197
    oatmeal cookies, 184
Peanuts
    banana fruit salad, 55
    green pea salad, 61
Peas
    salad, 61
    soup with zucchini, 78
    steaming time, 99
Pie crust, 206
Potatoes
    au gratin, 105

hash browned, 194
Parmesan, 106
salad, 61
scalloped, 107
soup, 79
steaming time, 99
Pumpkin pie blend, 32

R
Ratatouille, 127
Recommended reading, 234
Red snapper
    baked fish in cream sauce, 154
    fish stew, 77
    poached fish, 153
    stove-top fish, 156
    stuffed fish, 156
    with mushroom topping, 155
Rice
    curry, 115
    fried, 114
    saffron, 113
    Spanish, 114
    stuffed grape leaves, 211
    with parsley, 113
Ricotta cheese
    avocado spread, 41
    crêpes
        peach brandy, 199
        blackberry, 200
    fruit and cheese dessert, 182
    fruit salad, 55
    lasagna, 141
    stuffed manicotti, 140

S

Salad Dressings, 65—69
  Avocado Dressing, 67
  Blue Cheese Dressing, 66
  Buttermilk Tahini Dressing, 65
  Curry Yogurt Dressing, 65
  Dill Sesame Dressing, 69
  French Dressing, 66
  Louis Dressing, 68
  Mustard Sesame Dressing, 69
  Sesame Dill Dressing, 69
  Sesame Tahini Dressing, 68
  Simple Vinaigrette Dressing, 68
  Tart Cream Dressing, 66
  Thousand Island Dressing, 67
Salads, 53-65
  about, 53-54
  Almost Waldorf Salad, 56
  Arabian Salad, 63
  Banana-Peanut Fruit Salad, 55
  Basic Vegetable Salad, 57
  Bulghur Salad, 64
  Celery Seed Cabbage Salad, 59
  Coleslaw, 60
  Cucumber Stick Salad, 62
  Dill Tomatoes, 63
  Fettucine Salad with Mushrooms, 59
  Guy's Curry Vegetable Salad, 60
  Macaroni Salad, 58
  Peggy's Green Pea Salad, 61
  Pickled Mushrooms, 65
  Potato Salad, 61
  Ricotta and Fruit Salad, 55
  Shrimp and Macaroni Salad, 58
  Sour Cream Cucumbers, 62
  Spicy Citrus Salad, 56
  Spinach Salad, 57
  Tarragon Tossed Salad, 64
Salmon
  with caper sauce, 153
  log, 46
Sauces, 85—95
  about, 85-87
  Basic White Sauce, 88
  Bordelaise Sauce, 89
  Cheese Sauce, 88
  Creamy Herb Sauce, 90
  Curry Sauce, 88
  Dijon Sour Cream Sauce, 90
  Dill Horseradish Sauce, 91
  Hollandaise Sauce, 92
  Honey Mayonnaise, 93
  Mayonnaise, 93
  Mint Sauce, 91
  Miso Tahini Sauce, 90
  Quick Rarebit Sauce, 92
  Salsa, 94
  Teriyaki Sauce, 92
  Tofu Sesame Sauce, 93
  Tomato Sauce, 94
  Wine Mushroom Sauce, 89
  Wine Sauce, 88
Seeds, 29
Sesame butter (see tahini)
Shopping, 23

Shrimp
  creole, 157
  curry, 158
  macaroni salad, 58
  oyster bake, 160
  scampi, 159
  spread, 46
  stuffed artichokes, 128
Sole
  amandine, 154
  in cream sauce, 154
  poached, 153
  stuffed fish, 156
  with capers, 159
Soups, 71—83
  about, 71-73
  Broccoli Soup with Cheese and Ginger, 82
  Carrot Curry Soup, 74
  Cheese Soup, 77
  Corn Chowder, 78
  Cream of Broccoli Soup, 82
  Eggplant and Fresh Basil Soup, 74
  Fish Stew, 77
  Guy's 20-Minute Vegetable Stew, 83
  New England Clam Chowder, 75
  Potato Soup, 79
  Spinach Soup with Lemon, 79
  Tomato Soup, 75
  Tortilla Soup, 76
  Vegetable Miso Soup, 81
  Zucchini Chowder, 80
  Zucchini and Pea Soup, 78
Soy sauce (tamari), 33

Special seasonings, 34-35
Spices, 30-32
Spinach
  greens and grains, 121
  salad, 57
  soup with lemon, 79
  steaming time, 99
Spreads
  crab, 43
  cream cheese, 49, 50
  garbanzo sesame, 42
  garlic tofu, 42
  herb cheese ball, 49
  ricotta avocado, 41
  salmon log, 46
  shrimp, 46
  simplest, 38
  smoked oyster roll, 47
  tofu avocado, 41
  tofu egg salad, 40
Storage temperatures, 231

T

Tahini
  about, 29
  buttermilk dressing, 65
  cookies, 184
  dill sesame dressing, 69
  garbanzo sesame spread, 42
  miso sauce, 90
  mustard sesame dressing, 69
  sesame dressing, 68
  tofu sesame sauce, 93

Tamari (soy sauce), 33
Thickening agents, 86
Tofu
about, 33, 142-143
avocado spread, 41
cheesecake, 208
egg salad, 40
garlic spread, 42
lasagna, 141
sesame sauce, 93
stuffed manicotti, 140
Tofu Main Courses, 142—149
Creamy Tofu and Mushrooms, 149
Curried Tofu and Onions, 146
Sesame Tofu, 145
Sweet and Sour Vegetables and Tofu, 148
Teriyaki Tofu, 146
Tofu Burritos, 145
Tofu Patties, 147
Tofu Saute, 144
Tofu Tacos, 144
Tomatoes
cauliflower sauce for pasta, 136
dill, 63
salsa, 94
sauce, 94
squash saute, 124
Tools, kitchen, 20-22
Tricks of the trade, 232-235
Vegetable Accompaniments, 97—108
Au Gratin Potatoes, 105
Brussels Sprouts with Nutmeg, 106
Brussels Sprouts with Sour Cream, 102

Carrots with Tarragon, 103
Cooked Beets, 101
Debbie's Creamy Zucchini Curry, 108
Gingered Carrots and Broccoli, 103
Green Beans with Sunflower Seeds, 105
Lemony Apples and Carrots, 104
Mashed Potatoes, 102
Parmesan Potatoes, 106
Scalloped Potatoes, 107
Spicy Summer Squash, 108
Steamed Carrots, 104
Sunshine Cauliflower, 102
Tarragon Steamed Artichokes with Dill Dip,
101
Whipped Yams, 107

V

Vegetables, (also see names of vegetables)
about, 97-99
accompaniments 97-108
broth powder, 73
curry, 126
curry salad, 60
fried, with soba, 135
herb companions for, 31-32
steaming chart, 99
stew, 83
sweet and sour, with tofu, 148
Vegetable Main Courses,, 120—133
Cheese Fondue, 133
Chile Relleno Casserole, 131
Chinese Vegetables, 124
Eggplant Patties, 129

Enchiladas, 131
Fresh Tomato and Squash Saute, 124
Greens and Grains, 121
Mushrooms Paprika, 123
Mushroom Stroganoff, 122
Mushroom Tacos or Tostadas, 130
Quesadillas, 132
Ratatouille, 127
Sesame Eggplant, 129
Spicy Stir-fried Vegetables, 125
Stuffed Acorn Squash, 127
Stuffed Artichokes, 128
Vegetable Curry, 126

W

Waffles
    about, 187-188
    Belgian, 198
    peanut gingerbread, 197
Weights and measures, 229-231
Wine
    sauce, 88
    mushroom sauce, 89

Y

Yams
    candied, 210
    whipped, 107
Yogurt
    apple nut pancakes, 195
    curry dressing, 65
    peanut gingerbread waffles, 197
    shrimp curry, 158
    smoothie, 216

Z

Zucchini
    bread, 172
    chowder, 80
    curry, 108
    fresh tomato and squash saute, 124
    pancakes, 195
    pea soup, 78
    ratatouille, 127
    steaming time, 99

NOTES

About the Authors:

Susann Geiskopf and Mindy Toomay have come to this collaboration based on shared values, but from very different backgrounds. The past decade has seen Susann through four-and-a-half years of college, a stint as a kindergarten teacher, and the development of a thriving hat business. That same period has encompassed for Mindy several years as a professional editor and the beginning of a writing and publishing career. Among Susann's pleasurable pursuits are photography and embroidery. Mindy relaxes by quilting and is an avid reader and writer of poetry. They make time in their lives for gardening and periodic rejuvenating holidays. Both live in Sacramento, California. They met in 1971 and have since cooperated on numerous projects.